THIS
I KNOW
FOR SURE

BABBIE MASON

THIS

I KNOW
FOR SURE

Taking God at His Word

Abingdon Press

Nashville

THIS I KNOW FOR SURE

Copyright © 2013 by Abingdon Press

Library of Congress Cataloging-in-Publication Data

Mason, Babbie.
  This I know for sure / Babbie Mason.
    pages cm
  ISBN 978-1-4267-4081-7 (pbk. : alk. paper) 1. God (Christianity) 2. Spirituality. I. Title.
  BT103.M275 2013
  231.7—dc23

2013010803

To my sons, Gerald and Chaz,
who both reached landmark birthdays this year,
may you always know for sure,
beyond any shadow of a doubt,
that you are deeply loved by Jesus and me.

ACKNOWLEDGMENTS

Allow me to thank some very special people who helped this dream become a reality.

To Pamela Clements, Sally Sharpe, Susan Sally, Johnny Stephens, and my Abingdon family for your keen ability, tireless encouragement, and faithful friendship.

To my inner circle: Ruth, Donna, Benita, Barb, Vernessa, and Nancy. Thanks for journeying with me all these years.

To my brother, Pastor Ben Wade, and my Tithe Missionary Baptist Church family for the way you care.

To Charles, my dear husband. Nothing thrilled my heart more, after a long day of writing and recording, than the aroma of one of your home-cooked meals calling me to the kitchen, to your side, and to your heart. You make *home* one of my favorite words.

To my mother, Georgie Wade, and all the Wade family. Thanks for cheering me on. Like Dad always said, "If God be your partner, make your plans larger."

To Kimberly Hutchens, my personal assistant. Congratulations on ten years at Babbie Mason Ministries! I am so grateful for you!

To Jesus Christ, the Living Word, thank You for this humble privilege. I do have one more request. Would you please confirm in the heart of this dear reader, that with You, all things are possible?

CONTENTS

INTRODUCTION

This year I'm celebrating a landmark year in my life and ministry. God has blessed me to reach my thirty-year anniversary in ministry as a full-time vocation, *and* I've just marked my Year of Jubilee—fifty years of knowing Christ as my personal Lord and Savior. And even after all this time, I'm certain that God is not finished with me yet. My best and brightest days are ahead of me.

I really don't recall a time in my life that I didn't have an awareness of God and His powerful presence. I've known about Jesus all my life—really, I was going to church nine months before I was born! And I realize now that being raised in a Christian home was a wonderful gift from God. Because of that, I gave my life to Christ as a small child, and as a Baptist pastor's daughter, I spent all of my formative years hearing my father preach and teach the powerful truths of God's word. I began serving as the church pianist full-time by age nine and did so until the day I got married. I have spent all of my adult years in some form of ministry, whether it was serving in my dad's church, being involved in campus ministries in college, or singing and speaking from the stage. After all this time, I can truly say that every day of walking with Jesus has gotten sweeter and sweeter.

I don't consider myself a Bible scholar by any means, but because I grew up a preacher's kid and was involved in church all my life, I have been a student of the Bible for as long as I can remember. I love studying the Bible and discovering the life-changing truth that God speaks directly to us when we open the Bible. God's word has made all the difference in my life.

I've composed songs, written books, and sung about God for many years. I've studied God's ways and desired to do His will, and I love telling others about the Lord. However, after fifty years of knowing the Lord, and thirty years of globe-trotting in an itinerant ministry, the Lord has challenged me with this revelation: although I have known about Him all of my life, I have hardly begun to *really* know Him.

After all the years of discovery and all the opportunities to sing about Him and to tell others about Him, I have yet to understand fully who He is. Don't get me wrong. I realize, on the one hand, that I have been on the receiving end of so many of His wonderful blessings. My relationship with Jesus is strong and vibrant. God has certainly poured His blessings out on me. But I realize, on the other hand, that in a lot of ways, I have lived well beneath my privilege. I have struck out into the unknown far too many times on my own without fully consulting the Lord. My vision of His plans for me, in some instances, has been tremendously shortsighted. I've believed Him for far too little, and I've not asked Him for nearly enough. My moments with Him have been far too brief, and in our conversations, I've spent entirely too much time talking and not enough time listening. And although I say I trust Him, there have been times when my heart has been consumed with fear. When I go through difficult seasons, I sometimes wonder how I'll make it or whether the situation could possibly work out for good.

When it comes to knowing Christ, I realize that I have yet to scratch the surface! He is unfathomable. He is unexplainable. His thoughts are too glorious; His ways are too awesome. He is simply too great to be contained or fully understood. Fifty years down the road, I can look back over the course of my relationship with the Lord and see that He has been faithful to me, just as He was faithful to King David, Abraham, Moses, and so many others whose encounters I've read about. I've studied in God's word where the prophets found Him to be trustworthy. I read how Jesus' disciples got to know Him personally. Now I can add my testimony to theirs. God has proved Himself faithful to *me*! He has challenged me not just to know more about Him but to *know* Him more completely, more intimately.

This is what I've found to be true. The more I hold on to Him, the more I am able to let go—to fully trust Him. He wants me to believe every word He has spoken and take Him at His word without one hint of doubting or second-guessing. He wants me to place my complete and utter confidence in Him. And He has given me the charge to present this challenge to you as well.

Knowing God and taking Him at His word may seem like a

lofty venture, but don't be intimidated by the enormity of it all, my good friend. This encounter is less like a day-to-day project to be completed and more like a lifelong adventure to be experienced. No, you don't need to know everything about God to grow in your faith. You just need to have a fervent desire to get to the next step. No, you won't have all the answers. Sometimes it seems the more I discover about God, the more questions I have about Him. It's true. In life, you will have many questions with no answers. But can I encourage you? Don't fret over the stuff you don't know. Rest in the assurance that God knows about everything you *don't* know about. My hope is that during this adventure, you'll increase in your confidence in the Lord. Maybe you'll learn a bit too.

I wanted to write this book because my greatest hope is, as your knowledge and understanding of God increase, your trust in Him will rise. And should there be things we don't understand, my prayer is that together, we will find the confidence to trust Him with those issues. I know for a fact that God has the answer to every question about your family, your finances, and your future. He has the solution for every disappointment concerning your past and the discouragement you feel over your broken relationships. Your heavenly Father has all of that— every single thing—under control.

So, friend, it's time we stop fretting over what we *don't know* and celebrate what we *do know*. Because I'm here to tell you that it's what you *do know* for sure that really matters.

THIS I KNOW FOR SURE

I love landmarks. My favorites are stamped like picture postcards in my mind. There's New York City's towering Empire

State Building that stretches as high as the sky. There's the White House, standing grand and glorious on Pennsylvania Avenue in Washington, DC. There's San Francisco's majestic Golden Gate Bridge that spans the bay of Northern California. And every time I see a picture of Paris's Eiffel Tower, I wish my husband, Charles, and I could pack our bags, hop on a plane, and go back to our favorite sidewalk café at sunset to watch lovers stroll by.

What about you? Do you have a favorite landmark—a spot on a hill, a familiar building, or some other iconic structure that serves as a reminder or a point of reference? Do you get a new sense of confidence when you recognize a familiar landmark that helped you get your bearings and get back on course after a stint of being disoriented?

Not long ago I was thinking about the landmarks in my life: my relationship with Christ, my marriage, my family, my church, and my friends. I thought about the things that mattered most in my life and how well they have grounded me, and I was inspired to write the song "This I Know for Sure." This song resonates with me deeply and inspired this book, its companion Bible study, and the music project, all by the same name. The chorus of this song, which serves as the outline for this entire program, testifies to the landmarks that anchor my journey of faith:

> There is a God in Heaven
> And I am in His plan
> He will forsake me never
> My life is in His hands
> His boundless love will lead me
> As long as time endures
> Oh, this I know
> This I know for sure

These landmarks point to promises that God has given me in His word, and we'll keep coming back to these landmark promises during our time together. There are countless promises in the Bible, and each one has your name on it. We don't have enough room or time to mine for all of them in this book, but pray with me beginning now that we will do justice to the ones we do explore because I don't want you to miss hearing the voice of God in any area of your life.

Second Timothy 1:12 has been a source of strength and encouragement for me. This powerful verse is truly a great theme for our study: "I know whom I have believed, and am persuaded that he is able to keep that which I have committed unto him against that day."

The Apostle Paul wrote these words to his beloved disciple Timothy while Paul was imprisoned for preaching the good news of the gospel of Jesus Christ. In this, the last letter that he would pen before his death, Paul wrote from a dark, dank prison cell, encouraging Timothy to keep going in the faith, to never give up, to hope for the best, to be sure of his faith, to continue in the name of Christ.

In the same manner, I want to challenge you, dear one. Despite what you may be going through right now—disappointments or losses, setbacks or heartbreaks—you must not be moved by how you feel. You must not be swayed by what you see. You must not allow your circumstances to cause your faith to waver in any way. You may have many questions about your health. You may face a mountain of debt. Your heart may wrestle with fears about the future. Your marriage may be in deep trouble. You may battle with loneliness or fear. Or your children may not be walking with the Lord. But in the midst of it all you can find the strength to stand strong, without compromise, on what you know for sure.

And what do you know for sure? Remember Paul's words to Timothy because they are for you too. You'll need to remember them in the days ahead. When our journey is complete, my prayer is that you can say, beyond any shadow of a doubt and with conviction, that you can claim the truth of 2 Timothy 1:12 right down to the depths of your soul. I like how the Common English Bible brings home the meaning: "I know the one in whom I've placed my trust. I'm convinced that God is powerful enough to protect what he has placed in my trust until that day."

I'm praying that God will do the miraculous in your life as you see His word coming alive in you. Regardless of how you feel, begin to step out on the edge of your faith. As you do, I believe God will meet you right where you are to show you a side of Him you have never seen or even imagined. He wants you to know Him as the Apostle Paul described in Ephesians 3:17-19: "That Christ may dwell in your hearts by faith; that ye, being rooted and grounded in love, may be able to comprehend with all saints what is the breadth, and length, and depth, and height; and to know the love of Christ, which passeth knowledge, that ye might be filled with all the fulness of God."

Many years ago, I was in a hurry to catch a plane from Atlanta to Seattle. On the way to the airport, there was an accident on the expressway, and traffic was jammed, causing me to arrive with only a few minutes left to get to the gate. I almost missed the flight. Passengers had already boarded the plane, and the gate agent was about to close the door to the Jetway when I ran up to the counter, breathless and in a nervous tizzy. She had given my seat to another passenger, but thank goodness one available seat was left on the plane—in first class!

I had never flown first class before in my life, and I felt a touch out of place, sitting in the section mostly filled with businessmen. But it didn't take me long to get comfortable in the oversized, plush leather seat. I checked out all the buttons, bells, and whistles that adjusted the headrest and footrest, along with my own TV monitor that gave me the choice to view recently released movies or play popular word games.

Once we were at cruising altitude, the flight attendant came through the aisle and passed a neatly folded hot towel to each passenger in the first-class cabin. I was glad I waited and took a quick glance around the compartment to see other passengers using the white cotton towel to wipe their hands and not their tray tables! Before long, the flight attendant took up the towels and returned with a white linen tablecloth, silverware, and a small dish holding two small chicken drummettes. As she set the small saucer on my tray, I thought, *This is so wonderful! I'll eat this snack very slowly. Since I missed lunch, these two little drumsticks will have to last me awhile.* I was delightfully surprised when the attendant retrieved the dish and brought a hot en-trée with a salad, roll and butter, dessert, and coffee! I was so carried away that I had to catch myself before I nudged the man sitting next to me with my elbow.

After the meal, I reclined in my seat and started a new book I had brought on board. Before I could finish the first chapter, I dozed off to take a wonderful nap. By the time the flight landed I was happy, full, and well rested. Prior to that flight, I had been totally satisfied with sitting in coach, in a middle seat, along with my soft drink and peanuts. Boy, did that flight change my life! It opened my eyes to the personal comforts and amenities that passengers were enjoying up there behind the curtain. Af-ter that flight, I immediately joined the airline's frequent fliers' club so I could earn free upgrades and enjoy the rewards. Since then I've traveled both in the coach section and in the first-class section, and this is what I know for sure: I like traveling first class a whole lot better than coach.

In these pages, we're about to embark on a life-changing adventure together. Before long we'll be soaring up where eagles fly—high above fear and failure—traversing over all those things that have held us down for far too long. Let's not delay one moment longer. We are about to say good-bye to doubt and skepticism. We'll not be coming back to those places again. Just ahead of us are lives filled with a deeper faith and a greater trust in the Lord. My prayer for you and for me on this lifelong journey is that we will commit to knowing God intimately, through a personal relationship with Jesus Christ, and take Him at His word without wavering.

Sometimes the trip will be a bit unpredictable, but we're in good hands. Jesus is with us, and He knows the way because *He* is the Way. He is our guide, and we will look forward to becoming more like Him as we explore spiritual landmarks like faith, trust, love, hope, and confidence. From His vantage point, I believe we'll see these virtues as never before.

We're seatmates in first class on this flight, so we'll be enjoying all the rich and satisfying blessings that God has in store. Every part of this trek will be life-changing as we learn to take God at His word. Are you ready? Ready to shake off the past and move into the next season of your faith? This I know for sure: your best is yet to come as you discover that a life of confidence and trust in the Lord Jesus is the most exciting adventure of all.

THIS I KNOW FOR SURE

Words and Music by Babbie Mason

When life is uncertain
Questions come and go
I'll not be moved by how I feel
But trust in what I know

Chorus
There is a God in Heaven
And I am in His plan
He will forsake me never
My life is in His hands
His boundless love will lead me
As long as time endures
Oh, this I know
This I know for sure

When the days are cloudy
Skies are grey with rain
The storm will soon pass over
And I'll remember once again

Chorus

When the nights are lonesome
Fear comes with dismay
I find peace in His presence
And strength again to say

Chorus

Eyes grow dim then knees get weak
How quickly seasons change
But this one thing is constant
God's love remains the same

So when my years are golden
The sun is sinking low
I'll not be moved by how I feel
But trust in what I know

Chorus

PART ONE

———————

THERE IS A GOD IN HEAVEN

And I am in His plan
He will forsake me never
My life is in His hands
His boundless love will lead me
As long as time endures
Oh, this I know
This I know for sure

There's not a star whose twinkling light
Illumes the distant earth,
And cheers the solemn gloom of night,
But goodness gave it birth.

There's not a cloud whose dews distil
Upon the parching clod,
And clothe with verdure vale and hill,
That is not sent by God.

There's not a place in earth's vast round,
In ocean deep, or air,
Where skill and wisdom are not found;
For God is every where.

Around, beneath, below, above,
Wherever space extends,
There Heaven displays its boundless love,
And power with goodness blends.

—James C. Wallace[1]

CHAPTER 1

EMBRACING A DEFINING MOMENT

I thought about my life,
and I decided to follow your rules.
I hurried and did not wait
to obey your commands.
—Psalm 119:59-60 NCV

It was shaping up to be the perfect Sunday. The weather was gorgeous—warm and balmy, not a cloud in the sky. I was invited to sing that morning at a church not far from home in a nearby suburb of Atlanta, so my husband, Charles, and I had attended worship there.

After church Charles and I were heading to a friend's house, where I would celebrate Donna—one of my dearest friends in all the world as well as my songwriting buddy—by helping to throw her a bridal shower. I was on my way to partake of an afternoon of levity and laughter and celebrate one of the biggest moments in my friend's life, and I was enjoying light-hearted conversation with Charles, my man, my husband of thirty-three years. The day couldn't have been more special.

I was driving the car that day. Atlanta's traffic is always congested, even on a Sunday afternoon. I got off the freeway and stopped at the light at the end of the exit ramp. We sat in the center lane of traffic, my view to the left obstructed by a van. When the light changed to green, I was approaching the intersection when the driver of that van suddenly slammed on his brakes and laid on his horn. Instinct kicked in, and I slammed on my brakes as well. Just then, a car came racing from the left, speeding through the intersection, running the light. Had I not stopped precisely at the moment I did, had I been a few more inches into the intersection, that speeding vehicle that I never saw coming would have T-boned our car.

I sat frozen in the intersection, unable to move. All I could do was call on the name of Jesus. I shudder to think how things could have turned out so differently that day, but God in all His grace and mercy saw fit to spare our lives. There's no doubt in my mind that angels of protection were encamped around us that Sunday afternoon. In the next few moments and days, that incident replayed in my mind. That narrow miss thrust the issue of my mortality to the forefront, and I was forced to review my life. I wondered, *If those had been my final moments on earth and I had been ushered into eternity, would God have been pleased with the life I had lived?* I was not asking, *Would He have been pleased with the songs I've written or awards I've won or people I've met or places I've been?* Instead I pondered, *Would God have been pleased with me and my relationship with Him? Would He be pleased with how I've represented Him here on earth?*

Deep in my heart I want to live every day to the fullest, right up to the moment I breathe my last breath and then hear the Lord say, "Well done, good and faithful servant." One of the first questions I asked myself was not, *Am I ready to die?* No, I'm certain that if today were my last day on earth, I'd go home to heaven to be with Jesus. The question I faced was, *Am I really living the life God designed me to live?*

The words of Psalm 138:7 are a powerful reminder of how God raised up a hedge of protection for me and showed Himself strong in a very real way:

> Though I walk in the midst of trouble,
>   you preserve my life.
> You stretch out your hand against the anger of my foes;
>   with your right hand you save me. (NIV)

Dr. Ravi Zacharias, a well-known Christian author, theologian, and apologist of the Christian faith, said so aptly: "God is the shaper of your heart. . . . God does not display his work in abstract terms. He prefers the concrete, and this means that at the end of your life one of three things will happen to your heart: it will grow hard, it will be broken, or it will be tender. Nobody escapes."[1] Aware of this truth now more than ever before, I desire to yield my heart, tender and trembling, and place it in God's hands. Not only do I desire to know God's plan for my life here on earth, but I'm determined to see that plan through right up until my very last breath.

SO OTHERS WILL KNOW HIM

I recently heard a story that made me consider the confidence I have in God. It was art day in a kindergarten boy's class. As he took out his paints and brushes, he announced, "I'm going to color a picture of God."

"But no one knows what God looks like," responded his teacher.

"They will when I get finished," the little boy said with certainty.

I like that little fellow's attitude. He has a childlike confidence in God that is truly admirable. I'm a bit envious. I have prayed for that kind of gumption—for the gall to stick my neck out and paint God in big, bold colors.

That day of my near accident, I took inventory of my faith in Christ. I wondered, *Babbie, do you really love Jesus? Does your commitment to Him run deep, all the way down to the foundation of your soul?* Sure, I made Jesus my Savior a long time ago. But the close call at that intersection forced me to recommit every area of my life to Him all over again. I realize that this life God has given me and my relationship with Him that springs forth from it are precious. And out of that relationship comes my assignment to serve Him and others. In light of that revelation, average is just not good enough anymore. Jesus deserves only the best. I am determined to give Him what's right, not what's left.

The Apostle Paul says in Philippians 3:8-9, "Yes, everything else is worthless when compared with the infinite value of knowing Christ Jesus my Lord. For his sake I have discarded everything else, counting it all as garbage, so that I could gain Christ and become one with him" (NLT). To do anything less is to compromise. I was reminded that life is precious and today is a gift from God. What I do with today is my gift to Him. I am to take nothing for granted. Not my family, my friends, or my church. Not my work, my play, or my worship, not even my next breath, because all of it could be gone in an instant. I have a new sense of urgency and a desire to live with intent and purpose. There is a newfound hunger to live an authentic life. More than ever before, I pray that what happens when I'm onstage becomes an overflow of who I am when the lights go down and the music stops rolling. My prayer is that the Babbie Mason people see under the bright lights onstage is one and the same with the woman they see under the glaring fluorescent lighting of the grocery store.

I've asked God to grant me many more opportunities to say like that little boy in art class, "People will know what God looks like when I'm finished." There is a lifetime of work left for me to do. I'm still here, so it's evident that God is not finished with me yet.

LESS DOING, MORE BEING

David's prayer in Psalm 119:59-60 says,

> I thought about my life,
>   and I decided to follow your rules.
> I hurried and did not
>   wait to obey your commands. (NCV)

Sometimes we need a good old-fashioned reality check to get us on the right road, don't we? God is teaching me not to be so concerned about the work He has left for me to do. I've been way too obsessed with *doing the work*. I admit I have far too often worshiped my work. I confess the ministry at times has been an idol. And at times, I've been caught up in the things I've been able to accomplish, proud of my to-do list.

I now know that God is not the least bit impressed with my to-do list. Instead, with God's help, I am learning to be more concerned about *His* to-do list. There is a work God wants me to do. But I must not make that the priority. That moment revealed to me that God wants to do a greater work *in me*; God is more concerned about my *to-be* list. And the work He does in me is what I truly desire much more than anything He could ever do *for me*. If He doesn't do anything else for me, He's done enough. However, He's the God who never stops investing in us. He is always calling us to come up higher. Jesus opened my eyes to the awareness that He is shaping me and making me, on a daily basis, to be more like Him. The process of shaping and making is at times uncomfortable, even painful. But through that process, I become the person He wants me to be. And as I become the person He wants me to be, the doing will take care of itself.

THIS DEFINING MOMENT

If you could orchestrate the ideal last day of your life, what would it look like? Suppose that the lights on your life would go down by the end of tomorrow. How would you spend the remaining hours? Would you spend your time with family and loved ones? Would you spend it praying? Would you visit an aging parent? Would you hold your grandbabies? Perhaps you would throw a party, serve delicious food, dance, and celebrate with your family and friends. Would you say words you've been needing to say for a long time? Words like these: *I love you. I'm so sorry. Would you forgive me?*

I'm asking you not to wait for that one defining moment

that causes you to examine your life or your faith. Don't wait for the near miss to ask the Holy Spirit to shine His light on your heart. Instead, think about what if *this moment* was your defining moment?

In this moment, I'm challenging you to ask and allow God to examine your life and to show you how He wants you to draw near to Him. But don't get it wrong here. God doesn't use guilt to shame or to humble you. By His Holy Spirit, He draws you to Himself. With conviction and truth, He leads you to recognize it's time for change. And with His help, change is just a prayer away.

Begin by asking yourself very real, very pertinent questions:

Do I really love God as I say I do?
Do I really believe God's word?
Am I putting God's plan for my life into practice?
Where do my priorities lie?
Am I obsessed with my accomplishments?
Do I care more about impressing people than pleasing God?
Am I painting God in big, bold colors for all the world to see?

Take the time to digest these questions and answer with an honest spirit. What is God revealing to you? Where do you feel His presence urging you to draw close to Him? As you wrestle with these questions and open yourself up to where God is leading, prepare your mind. Decide that you will be honest and transparent with God, giving Him permission to do His work in you. Then prepare your heart. Be honest with yourself by submitting yourself to God and receive the fresh start He offers you.

If your response is, "Lord, I'm not sure how to do this, but I'm ready to make the first step toward becoming the person You want me to be," that's the perfect starting place. If you're ready to shore up your faith in Christ, boost your confidence in His word, strengthen your resolve, embolden your witness, raise your hopes, and increase your desire to paint God in big, bold colors, then embrace this defining moment. This I know for sure: there's no better time than the present to begin.

CHAPTER 2

ESTABLISHING CONFIDENCE IN GOD

The eyes of the LORD move to and fro
throughout the earth that He may strongly
support those whose heart is completely His.
—2 Chronicles 16:9 NASB

Do you have close, intimate friends with whom you share
your life? Would you say that it is important to you not
only to know the basic facts about your close friends but also
to know how they think and feel? No doubt, you've shared
your heart with these friends in a way that has made your life
richer and more meaningful. Most likely you trust these friends

enough to be real and transparent with them, sharing laughter in the good times and sadness in times of loss.

God wants you to know Him the very same intimate way. He wants you to put aside any preconceived ideas about who you think He is or who you've been told He is and discover who He *really* is. Think about it. You probably don't trust people you don't know. You may be skeptical of people you are not familiar with until they prove themselves. But there is no reason to be skeptical of God. You can be completely confident in your relationship with Him by becoming familiar with Him through His word and your experience with Him.

Before that defining moment at the intersection that Sunday afternoon, I was pretty certain of my goals in life. As a take-charge person, I knew that I could achieve anything I wanted if I worked hard enough to get it. After that near miss, I realized that I can control absolutely nothing in my life. Everything—and *anything*—about my life could change in an instant! The only certainty, the only praiseworthy quality concerning me, is *Jesus*. Achieving my goals is no longer important. Knowing God more intimately and realizing His purpose for me are the only things that matter.

CONFIDENCE IN GOD'S PROVIDENCE

I remember a time, almost thirty years ago, when I was a middle school music teacher. I was at a crossroads in my life, trying to decide whether to remain as a teacher or quit my job and step out in faith to pursue a growing music ministry. Charles and I had been married a few years, and we were already raising a family of growing boys. The word had begun to spread about my singing, and I received invitations to visit churches and civic groups on weekends and over the summer months. Little by little my calendar filled up with singing invitations, but I was still hesitant to leave the security of my day job. Deep in my heart, the Lord knew that I dreamed of launching a music ministry as a full-time vocation. But that wasn't possible or practical because Charles had started his own small business, and my position as a teacher gave us the health benefits we needed. Together, Charles and I prayed about me quitting my job. I sought the advice of family and friends and the counsel of our pastor, but ultimately the decision was mine to make.

One night my dear friend Barb dropped by for a visit. She wanted me to meet an evangelist friend and his wife. We chatted for a while, and before we ended our conversation, the evangelist asked if I had any prayer requests. I excitedly told him about my desire to quit my job and my reluctance to leave. He prayed a simple prayer, and I said, "Amen," believing that God had heard our requests. Then an amazing thing happened. That evangelist, whom I met only moments before, volunteered to buy our health insurance for a solid year so I could quit my job without any concerns. What a mighty God I serve! Truly, God can open up a sea and provide a way where there seems to be no way.

I shared with you earlier how the Lord inspired me to compose the song "This I Know for Sure." The first verse and chorus are so appropriate for this moment:

When life is uncertain
Questions come and go
I'll not be moved by how I feel
But trust in what I know

Now, here is the chorus.

There is a God in Heaven
And I am in His plan
He will forsake me never
My life is in His hands
His boundless love will lead me
As long as time endures
Oh, this I know
This I know for sure

I'm here to tell you that there is a God in heaven, and He is powerful enough to provide a way for you. I'm sure of it! I know this because He provided a way for me, and His word constantly assures us of His attention and provision.

CONFIDENCE IN GOD'S POWER

There was a man who was certain that God could make a way for him. Daniel was a man of noble lineage, but more than that, he was a man of noble character. (Now, as we talk about him, I want to challenge you to dismiss the old notions you might have about God and His word. You've probably heard the story of Daniel in the lions' den, but don't just take a casual glance at this Bible story. Don't tune out now, or you'll miss out! The Bible is as relevant today as it was thousands of years ago. Ask God to help you see this timeless story with brand-new eyes.)

Daniel was a brilliant man who had found favor with God and kings because of his excellent character and keen ability to conduct himself in governmental matters. Daniel was a great man before his God, and God exalted him before men. King Darius was so impressed with Daniel's integrity and dedication to service that he appointed Daniel as one of his three administrators and planned to put Daniel over the affairs of the entire kingdom of Babylon.

Jealous because of Daniel's promotion, other administrators and officials tried to dig up dirt concerning Daniel's character, but read what the book of Daniel says concerning this:

> The administrators and the satraps tried to find grounds for charges against Daniel in his conduct of government affairs, but they were unable to do so. They could find no corruption in him, because he was trustworthy and neither corrupt nor negligent. Finally these men said, *"We will never find any basis for charges against this man Daniel unless it has something to do with the law of his God."* (6:4-5 NIV, emphasis mine)

Can you see that no ground is sacred to your enemies? These evil men conspired against Daniel and convinced King Darius to issue and enforce a law saying that anyone who prays to any god or man, except the king, would become dinner for a den of lions. Daniel, a man of lionhearted valor, would rather disobey the king's edict than dishonor his God.

Daniel was a man of great power because he was a man of great prayer. Pay attention to how he continued to live his life. Even after the edict had been decreed, Daniel openly defied it with the same fervor he had always demonstrated. He continued to pray three times daily with his window open toward Jerusalem, his homeland. He even fashioned a room in his home for this routine act of devotion. The great preacher and author Charles Spurgeon said of Daniel, "I don't know how you find it, but there are some of us who never pray so well as by the old arm-chair."[1]

Daniel was not ashamed of his godly heritage, and he was not ashamed of his God. He wanted to do right by pleasing God with his life. But his enemies saw to it that Daniel would put his life on the line for what he believed. He demonstrated that just because we are living for God doesn't mean that everything is always going to go smoothly. After all, hundreds of years later, Jesus would be brutally beaten and nailed to a cruel Roman cross. And He did nothing wrong. What makes us think we can escape unscathed? Life will not always be easy, but God always remembers the names of those who dedicate their lives to Him.

Daniel was sentenced to the lions' den, and into the den he went! After spending an entire night with lions and angels, he came out the next morning without so much as a kitten's scratch. But not so for his accusers, who were all, along with their wives and children, thrown to the den of hungry lions. All were consumed before they could hit the ground. What became of Daniel? He was hailed as a celebrity. The king admired him, the people applauded him, and God honored him.

CONFIDENCE IN GOD'S PRESENCE

So what's the moral of the story? That you and I would know God like Daniel knew God. The heart of the matter is that God is looking for people with strong confidence in Him. He is searching for people who not only believe *in* Him but also *believe Him* and will keep on believing Him no matter what circumstances they face.

He's looking for you, dear friend. Have you opened wide the window of your heart to look His way? He's searching for someone He can depend on no matter what may come. Second Chronicles 16:9 reminds us of the kind of people that God is looking for, "The eyes of the LORD move to and fro throughout the earth that He may strongly support those whose heart is completely His" (NASB).

There's so much to learn from Daniel's life. Let me highlight this: I will never discount the power of God's presence. No matter how deep my pit of despair may be, the arm of God's grace is longer still. No matter how much people let me down, Jesus will always lift me up. Sometimes I find myself staring at a mountain of problems, and I wonder how in the world I'm going to climb it. But God reminds me that there's no problem or situation He can't handle. There is nothing going on in my life that has Him stumped. There's not a relationship problem, financial challenge, health struggle, or personal battle that God can't win.

BUILDING CONFIDENCE IN GOD

So how do we build our confidence and trust in God? First, we must acknowledge that no one can know God completely. The Bible says,

> "My thoughts are not your thoughts,
>   neither are your ways my ways,"
>   declares the Lord.
> "As the heavens are higher than the earth,
>   so are my ways higher than your ways
>   and my thoughts than your thoughts." (Isaiah 55:8-11 NIV)

Let me encourage you not to obsess about the things you *don't* know; I think we let the stuff we don't know occupy too much of our daily thought process. For instance, you might be preoccupied with what you're going to wear tomorrow or what to fix for dinner. You might be concerned about whether you'll qualify for a home loan or if your car will make it to work. You might be stressed, worrying whether the kids will get over their colds or how you'll pay the taxes. We worry way too much about the things we cannot control. Too often we speculate and theorize and even play out imaginary scenarios in our minds over what *might* happen. Well, what *might* happen and what the Lord's plan *is* are two totally different things. Remember, God is in control. And that takes us back to our main theme. Trust in what you already know, then leave the rest to God.

How do you start? Here are three ways to increase your confidence in God:

1. *Don't confuse facts and feelings.* Base your feelings on facts, not your facts on feelings. You can *be* confident without *feeling* confident. You can even make a mistake and still be confident to start over. You can fall flat on your face and still find the confidence in the Lord to get up and try again. You may have a question, but you can find the confidence to look for answers. Your confidence does not come as a result of your success; your confidence comes from knowing the Lord. Remember these words of Isaiah:

   > He will be your safety.
   > He is full of salvation, wisdom, and knowledge.
   > Respect for the LORD is the greatest treasure. (33:6 NCV)

2. *Don't get caught up in what other people are doing.* A good way to have a car accident is to focus too long on what another driver is doing. Stay in your lane! Be careful not to allow the successes of others to distract you from what God has called you to do. Becoming distracted is a sure way to become defeated. Stay focused on the assignment He has given *you*. This powerful promise from God's word is like a billboard on the highway: "So let's keep focused on that goal, those of us who want everything God has for us" (Philippians 3:15 *THE MESSAGE*).

3. *Don't make excuses for yourself.* You might say, "I'm too old." Not true! Daniel was eighty years old when he was thrown to the lions. You could be thinking, *I'm too young.* I beg to differ! You are never too young to be used by God. Mary, the mother of Jesus, was a young teenager when she gave birth to our Lord Jesus. You might say, "I'm different." No, you're not different. You're unique! There's much more value in being unique. You might say, "I'm just a housewife," or "I'm just a janitor," or "I'm just a grocery store clerk." You are not "just" an anything! You are a child of God! You are valuable and precious to Him. You're worth it! He has a unique and beautiful plan for you. Proverbs 14:26 tells us that "in the fear of the LORD there is strong confidence, / And his children will have refuge" (NASB).

Today, be mindful not to be overwhelmed by all the things you don't know. Instead, remember *who* you know. How can you begin to know God better? It's like looking at a huge mountain stretched out in front of you and wondering, *How in the world will I ever begin to climb it? Where and how do I begin such a task?*

The answer, my friend is this: take it one step at a time. This I know for sure: the difference between the possible and the impossible is determined by your confidence in God.

CHAPTER 3

ENJOYING YOUR IDENTITY

Being confident of this very thing, that he which hath begun a good work
in you will perform it until the day of Jesus Christ.
—*Philippians 1:6*

I never thought I could fall in love again. Then the grand-children were born. Precious and Punkin', as I call them, are my reward for getting older. I love when they come to our house for a visit. One day our granddaughter, five years old at the time, crawled into my lap to get the kind of tender loving care that only a grandmother can give. (Eskimo kisses are our favorite.) We had just finished rubbing noses when my granddaughter said in her sweet manner, "Grammy, now I see where my daddy gets his nose!" She was right. No doubt about it. Her daddy gets his nose from me. Although it was a bit backhanded, I took it as a compliment.

YOU LOOK JUST LIKE YOUR FATHER

Do your kids have your trademark brown eyes or dry sense of humor? Did they inherit your artistic ability or your love for sports? It doesn't matter if you're a parent or not. No doubt you've seen similarities between you and your parents. Have you ever looked at a family photo only to realize those striking inherited traits? I've seen it in my family for sure. I can trace those almond-shaped eyes, high cheekbones, and that perpetual widow's peak all the way back to my great-grandfather. And I can see the traits in the families of others I've met along the way.

One Sunday evening, I had just finished delivering a concert, and I headed for the lobby to greet concertgoers. There I met a mom and dad with three beautiful children. I had to laugh out loud. The entire family sported curly red hair, freckles, and glasses. Down here in the South, folks say that children "take after" their parents. Sometimes others recognize the resemblance before you do. You've probably heard your friends say with a certainty, "There's no way you can deny that child. Why, she's a chip off the ol' block!"

The same can be said of us and our resemblance to our Father, God. There is something we humans possess that separates us from all of God's other creatures. God made us with the ability to relate to Him and others on a spiritual level. We bear His mark by virtue of the fact that we have a changed nature. We take after Him in the way we act, by the words we say, through our personalities, by the love we share, and through our ability to worship Him. Others are sure to say, "No doubt about it. She's a child of God." And like fabric in the hands of a tailor who cuts away everything that doesn't look like a suit, our Father molds us and shapes us into His image, taking away anything that doesn't resemble Him.

REALIZING YOUR IDENTITY

On this leg of our journey, we've been talking about finding confidence in Christ. There is a lifetime of joy waiting for those who have realized a deep peace and assurance in knowing who God has created them to be. Not a vain, conceited haughtiness or self-reliance because you'll never find real, authentic confidence to be who you were born to be by looking within yourself. You cannot will it through determination or dredge it up through positive thinking. You might say, "Well, Babbie, I must be a Christian. I'm a good person. I go to work every day. I take care of my family. I go to church on Sundays. I even volunteer at the local PTA." Although those things are good, they do not make you a child of God. No, dear friend, there is only one way you can discover who you are meant to be: you must first have a relationship with Jesus. Without Him, you are empty inside. You see, confidence in your spiritual life isn't found in self-reliance, vanity, or inner motivation. Confidence is a person, and that person is Jesus. When you discover who Christ is—and are confident of His presence and power in your life—you begin to discover who you are.

So, who are you, way deep down inside? Who do you resemble? Far too often, this question is difficult to answer because we tend to allow other people to become our points of reference.

I've made the mistake of comparing myself to others, or worse yet, I've granted people permission to define who I was instead of allowing God to define my identity. Have you permitted people to offer their opinions or to pass judgment, deeming you beautiful or not beautiful, acceptable or unacceptable, fit or unfit? The problem is that people's standards and opinions are constantly changing. It's a system that is set up for failure. When you allow others to define you, you can be sure you will never quite measure up. You will always fall short. You will always feel less than enough. That, my friend, is giving people too much power over your life.

A STORY OF TWO SISTERS

One dear sister in the Bible was slow to realize the powerful truth that a strong identity and inner confidence come from God and not from the validation of others. This dear one's name was Leah. She was the older daughter of Laban, and her story is found in Genesis 29. We'll begin with verses 16-20:

> Laban had two daughters: the name of the elder was Leah, and the name of the younger was Rachel. Leah was tender eyed; but Rachel was beautiful and well favoured. And Jacob loved Rachel; and said, I will serve thee seven years for Rachel thy younger daughter. And Laban said, It is better that I give her to thee than that I should give her to another man: abide with me. And Jacob served seven years for Rachel; and they seemed unto him but a few days, for the love he had to her.

Oh, the power of love! Here is a man who is willing to work seven long years of backbreaking labor for the woman he loved. You've heard the old adage that says, "Love is blind." I like to say, "Love is blind. It is also deaf and mute." Jacob had fallen in love with Rachel, and I don't think he would have noticed if he had been dropped on his head. Love deprived the man of all of his senses.

Anyway, back to Leah. The Bible tells us that "Leah was tender eyed" (Genesis 29:17). Some biblical reference books define the word *tender* as meaning "delicate" or "soft." Other references use the words *weak* or *dull* and say that her eyes "had no sparkle." One source uses the word *nice*. Now, no girl that I know ever considers the word *nice* a favorable compliment. Some say that Leah, the older sister, was matronly and frumpy, a bit gawky with lightly colored eyes. The name Leah means "cow." So any way you look at it, she lacked the feminine features that we consider beautiful and desirable, compared to her younger sister, Rachel—beautiful, stunning, gorgeous, youthful Rachel.

If Rachel were living today, she'd more than likely be well suited for Hollywood's silver screen. It's easy to imagine why every woman desired to be like her while every man wanted to be with her. Especially Jacob, who was Laban's nephew. He had recently arrived at his Uncle Laban's home, and his heart was set on having Rachel as his wife from the moment he laid eyes on her. It seemed to be a match made in heaven. The Hollywood beauty and the new kid on the block seemed perfect for each other. But we know that when relationships are based on outward appearances alone, the love affair teeters on shaky ground. For him, it was love at first sight. For her, she was blown away by breath and britches. Jacob would stop at nothing until the day that Rachel would become his bride.

Laban liked the idea of having a robust, good-looking son-in-law to marry his daughter, and it didn't hurt to have a strong back to help with the herds. The two men agreed. Jacob would work for Laban for seven years. When that seven-year stint was complete, Jacob and Rachel were to be married. So Jacob said to his father-in-law, "Give me my wife. My time is completed, and I want to make love to her" (Genesis 29:21 NIV). It was customary in those days, on the evening of the wedding, that the heavily veiled bride was brought into the darkened bridal chamber and presented to her husband. All the wine that Jacob drank at the marriage banquet must have gone to his head, for surely if he had been sober he would have been aware of Laban's bait and switch.

Certainly he would have distinguished the difference between Leah and Rachel. Jacob had been engaged to Rachel for seven years and was smitten by her in every way. So, even in the dark of night, it seems a man who is deeply in love could at least recognize his wife's voice. It leaves you to wonder whether Leah was a willing coconspirator in this charade. Imagine her whispers of sweet nothings into Jacob's ear at the risk of being discovered. Being the older daughter and yet unmarried, it's quite possible that Leah was just as excited to seize the moment as her father was. (Dishonesty and trickery seem to have worked their way all through this dysfunctional family. Jacob tricked his brother, Esau, out of his birthright. Read the story in Genesis 25:29-34. Then Jacob, with the help of his mother, Rebekah, deceived his father, Isaac, and took his brother's blessing. Their story is in Genesis 27.) The sordid details are the makings of a television network miniseries. Either way, Jacob's marriage was consummated, but it wasn't until the next morning and the effects of much wine had worn off that Jacob realized he had not slept with Rachel. Instead, Leah was his bride.

Jacob was furious! Reluctantly, he agreed to work for Laban for seven more years. At the conclusion of Leah's bridal week, Laban also gave Rachel to Jacob as his wife. Jacob became the husband of two wives at the same time, a custom permitted in those days. But the Bible stated that "Jacob made love to Rachel also, and his love for Rachel was greater than his love for Leah" (Genesis 29:30 NIV). Thus began the battle between the sisters. These two women, having to share the same husband, found themselves in a head-to-head competition for the man they both loved. However, Leah found herself in the painful position of having to fight to win the affections of a man who loved her sister much more.

One way to get Jacob to love her, Leah thought, was to give him children. In the Hebrew culture, parents prayed and asked God for just the right name—a name that would typify the kind of life they envisioned the child would lead. This is very significant as we look closely at the names Leah gave her children. Let me give you the rundown on them:

The first child, a son, was Reuben, meaning "God has noticed my trouble." Leah said, "Jehovah has noticed my trouble—now my husband will love me" (Genesis 29:32 TLB).

The second child was a son, Simeon, meaning "Jehovah heard." Leah said, "Jehovah heard that I was unloved, and so he has given me another son" (Genesis 29:33 TLB).

The third child was another son, Levi, meaning "attachment." Desperately, Leah said, "Now at last my husband will become attached to me, because I have borne him three sons" (Genesis 29:34 NIV).

Let me interject a bit of reality right here to ask you a question. Can you hear the cries of rejection from Leah's heart? Real rejection is when you love a man, but he doesn't love you back. Real rejection is when you conjure up the nerve to say those three words, "I love you," only to be left hanging. Real rejection is when you give your money, your time, and your heart only to come up empty. That, my friend, is what it means to be dissed—disrespected, disregarded, disenchanted, dismissed. I'd say this could do damage to a woman's confidence and cause her to have an identity crisis for sure. I can imagine Leah's frustrated conversation aimed at Jacob in the evening just before bed. "Hey, Jake! What am I, chopped liver over here? I cook your meals. I'm a great wife and mother. I give you plenty of good lovin'. I give you many sons to bear your name. You could at least tell me you love me! What's up with this?" Ever been there? Can you feel Leah's pain? More important, can you see a pattern here? Insanity is doing the same thing again and again expecting different results.

Try as she might, Leah's efforts were futile. She grew weary of trying to win Jacob's love and approval. It was then she came to the end of herself. Sister Leah finally heard the wake-up call. But it was not too late. Because when God is in the picture, it's never too late!

Leah had a fourth son, named Judah, meaning "praise." She said, "Now I will praise Jehovah!" (Genesis 29:35 TLB). And then she stopped having children.

Well, she stopped having children for a while anyway. Sometimes old habits die hard. Amen? Leah would have more children for Jacob. He also had children with his wife Rachel and his wives' handmaidens Zilpah and Bilhah. Is it any wonder that this family would later be torn apart with bitterness, anger, strife, and jealousy?

I WANT TO LOOK LIKE MY FATHER

So what can we take away from this saga of two sisters?

First of all, *there is always a danger when we compare.* I know what it feels like to compare oneself to others. I've tried to sing like other singers or write a song like other writers. But when I tried to be someone else, I was missing. And I was dishonoring God. I learned that just being myself is far better than trying to be a replica of someone else. Leah learned that too. Yes, Rachel was the beautiful one with the sophisticated ways. But Leah, not Rachel, gave birth to Judah, through whose bloodline our Savior, Jesus, came. God had a plan for Leah, and He has a plan for you. We can know true peace when we stop comparing ourselves to everyone else, decide that we will trust the plan God has for each of us, and heed these words: "The LORD is my strength and my shield; my heart trusted in him, and I am helped: therefore my heart greatly rejoiceth; and with my song will I praise him" (Psalm 28:7).

Second, *it is always detrimental when we compete.* God has something wonderful in store for you! What God has for you, no one can take away from you. Though Leah was in some ways despised by her husband, God highly regarded her. Her sons would represent six of the twelve tribes of Israel. We can learn a significant lesson from Leah's story: cease striving and being anxious. Rest in the promise that God will finish the work He started in us. Remember this powerful truth from Philippians 1:6: "Being confident of this very thing, that he which hath begun a good work in you will perform it until the day of Jesus Christ." He will not leave you stranded to go it alone. He won't let you slip between the cracks or forget about your circumstances. You are God's very own, uniquely created to express His love in the earth.

Last, *there is always a downside when we compromise.* You always come out on the losing end when you sell out or lower your standards. God's plan will never require you to compromise the truth of His word. Do you know anyone who is a people pleaser? Those kinds of people express an inward need for love and acceptance and go to great lengths to please others to gain that love and acceptance, even if it goes against their inner convictions. This is not God's will. You can walk in a way that is pleasing to God. When you do this, you please Him and bring respect to yourself. You can know for sure that God is on your side, leading and guiding you every step of the way: "For it is God which worketh in you both to will and to do of his good pleasure" (Philippians 2:13).

Dear friend, I wholeheartedly believe that God's word is true. You can take Him at His word when He says that He has a perfect plan for your life. God wants to do the unbelievable in your life if you'll only believe Him for it. This I know for sure: there is a God in heaven, and when your confidence is solely in Him, you can embrace who you are without a hint of apology, accept yesterday without a twinge of guilt, enjoy today without an ounce of reservation, and anticipate tomorrow with a heart filled with hope.

PART TWO

———————

THERE IS A GOD IN HEAVEN

And I am in His plan

He will forsake me never
My life is in His hands
His boundless love will lead me
As long as time endures
Oh, this I know
This I know for sure

LORD, help me to resign
My doubting heart to thee,
And, whether cheerful or distressed,
Thine, thine alone to be.

My only aim be this,—
Thy purpose to fulfil,
In thee rejoice with all my strength,
And do thy holy will.

Lord, thy all-seeing eye
Keeps watch with sleepless care;
Thy great compassion never fails;
Thou hear'st my humble prayer.

So will I firmly trust
That thou wilt guide me still,
And guard me safe throughout the way
That leads to Zion's hill.

—Anonymous[1]

CHAPTER 4

FOLLOWING GOD'S LEAD

I am the way,
the truth, and the life:
no man cometh unto the Father,
but by me.
—John 14:6

My family loves to fish. When I was a child, my family spent many summer vacations fishing in the Great Lakes and the rivers and streams of Michigan and eastern Canada. It didn't matter if we fished from a boat, along the banks, or from a bridge. We fished in shallow streams and deep rivers with live and artificial bait, with rods and reels and cane poles. We didn't mind if the fish were large or small. We weren't concerned if the fish weren't biting. We just found a different spot and kept fishing. Catch and release, you say? What's that? If it was big enough to keep, it was big enough to eat.

On one vacation we took the family camper for a week's worth of fishing in eastern Ontario, Canada. We arrived at the campsite by midday, and everyone was eager to pitch in and get the site set up before evening. Afterward, Dad and Uncle Joe ventured out to find a grocery store to buy food, a few supplies, and fishing bait. When they hadn't returned by dusk, we grew concerned. Eventually Dad and Uncle Joe returned after dark and immediately launched into their story.

On the way to the store, the duo enjoyed the view of the pristine green Canadian landscape. The area around the campsite was densely wooded except for a nearby Indian burial ground and museum that featured the remains of Indian chieftains and historic artifacts. They found the store, did some shopping, and were headed back to the campsite when they took a wrong turn and got lost. They stopped at a gas station for directions, but neither Dad nor Uncle Joe could remember the name of the campground, the road it was on, or the direction it was in. Frustrated, they didn't know what to do. Then the gas station owner asked a key question: "Can you remember any signs or landmarks you saw along the way?"

Dad's face lit up like a Christmas tree as he retold the story. Dad, never off duty from preaching or teaching, always seeing natural events from a spiritual perspective, said, "Oh yes, now I remember! Our campsite is near some dry bones!"

The gas station owner recognized the description of the Indian burial ground and museum and sent them in the right direction. That day, Dad's reference to Ezekiel 37 was not just an Old Testament story but a road map to his destination.

Have you, like Dad and Uncle Joe, ever ventured on a trip with sketchy directions? If you have, then you know how that situation is a setup for a setback. Without a well-thought-out plan, you'll find yourself going around in circles, wasting precious time, energy, and resources. Thank goodness my family members knew the value of stopping to ask for help. The same is true in life. To reach your destination safely, you'll need personal assistance, a road map, and landmarks along the way to help you navigate the rough terrain and blind curves ahead.

One of God's most beautiful landmark promises is found in Jeremiah 29:11: " 'I know the plans I have for you,' declares the LORD, 'plans to prosper you and not to harm you, plans to give you hope and a future' " (NIV). The prophet Jeremiah wrote this to encourage the Jewish people who were living in exile, forced from their homeland by the Babylonian Empire. When Jeremiah wrote these words, he was reminding God's people of very important principles when searching for God's direction. He reminded them that times would change. People would change. Circumstances would change. But God and His promises never change, and these promises are still applicable to your life today.

God has a specific blueprint for your life, and He's taken the guesswork out of executing that plan by giving you His promise to lead you. There's no way you can know every detail about tomorrow, but you can trust God because He's already there. He sees His intended destination for you with no problem. So you may as well exchange worry for anticipation and get ready to enjoy the ride of your life!

As we seek to know *God intimately through a personal relationship with Jesus Christ and to take Him at His word without wavering,* God's word provides everything we need for the journey. Hebrews 12:1 tells us to lay aside all encumbrances, to run life's race with determination: "We are surrounded by a great cloud of people whose lives tell us what faith means. So let us run the race that is before us and never give up" (NCV).

When you falter, claim these words: "I know whom I have believed, and am persuaded that he is able to keep that which I have committed unto him against that day" (2 Timothy 1:12). This is not the time for an I-think-so or I-hope-so kind of thinking; this is the time for an I-know-so kind of faith. Life is too precious for you to miss what really matters, and what really matters is this: God loves you, and He has a plan for you that far exceeds your wildest dreams and imagination. And when you discover God's plan, your life will bring glory to Him. He guarantees it: "As it is written, Eye hath not seen, nor ear heard, neither have entered into the heart of man, the things which God hath prepared for them that love him" (1 Corinthians 2:9).

God desires to make the pathway plain that leads to His plan. You need only trust the road map.

ASK FOR DIRECTION

To know God's direction for your life, you must begin at the start. You'll know God's best only by coming face-to-face with the fact that, without direction, you'd be truly lost. Jesus said of Himself, "I am the way, the truth, and the life: no man cometh unto the Father, but by me" (John 14:6). *THE MESSAGE* translation puts it this way: "I am the Road, also the Truth, also the Life. No one gets to the Father apart from me." Does that paint a marvelous visual image in your mind?

With Jesus, a real, vibrant, and life-giving Christian walk is in store. Being a Christian is not about making an obligatory visit to church on Sunday morning. Church pews are filled with folks who go to church because of tradition or because it's the social thing to do. That's nothing more than cold, lifeless religion. There's so much more in store for you than that!

Jesus cares about your life—every single detail of it—the mortgage, the laundry, the grocery list, your job, your bank account, the baby in diapers, and the kid in college. Jesus wants to be involved in every aspect of your life, not just those things you decide to make Him a part of. So don't get caught up in dividing your life into sacred and secular compartments. For the believer, there is no such thing as sacred thinking and secular thinking. There is no such thing as your church life and the rest of your life. Jesus doesn't want you to come home from church and put your Christian life on the shelf with your Bible. He wants you to put it to use! Everything is sacred when you live for Christ. Jesus wants to be Lord of all, or He is not Lord at all. But He has not left you alone on the journey. Got questions about life? God's got answers: "When you call on me, when you come and pray to me, I'll listen. When you come looking for me, you'll find me" (Jeremiah 29:12-13 THE MESSAGE).

GET IN THE LANE

As a singer, conference speaker, and TV talk show host, I spend a great deal of time in my car. When Willie Nelson wrote the song "On the Road Again" he must've seen me waving to him from the passing lane. Before I walk out the door for a trip, I make sure I have reliable directions in my hand.

Have you ever trusted directions that proved to be unreliable? There's nothing more frustrating than having directions that don't make sense. That's always a possibility when you put your ultimate trust in others. In that scenario, you are one turn from impending disaster. You could end up going around in circles, wind up on a dead-end street, or be stranded alongside the highway. But when you let Jesus lead you, you're certain to avoid pitfalls and potholes. Jesus will never lead you astray.

If you've heard me speak at all, you've probably heard me talk a lot about my dad, Reverend Willie G. Wade. As if you couldn't tell, I'm a daddy's girl. Dad was the founding pastor of the Lily Missionary Baptist Church in Jackson, Michigan, and pastored there nearly forty years. (I was hired as the church's full-time pianist and choir director before my feet could barely reach the piano's pedals, so you can imagine that Dad and I spent lots of time together.) One of the saddest days of my life was March 4, 1986. That was the day Daddy passed away. That Wednesday night, just before prayer meeting, Dad sat down and took his last breath. When I received the news, it was as if my heart had been ripped out. I actually felt as if there was a hole in my chest from grief. But the Lord has sustained me, and I know that even though my dad is gone, the faithful legacy he left our family is firmly established. As a matter of fact, my faith is strengthened because I have the hope, a confident expectation of good, that reminds me that God is faithful and heaven is for real. Nothing is lost when you know where to find it.

Jesus commands that I not be discouraged, throw in the towel, and quit when times get tough. When it comes to life's challenges, I've learned this: it may not be OK right now, but it's going to be all right. The psalmist David wrote, "I have been young, and now am old; yet I have not seen the righteous forsaken, nor his descendants begging bread" (Psalm 37:25). Experience leads me to believe that chances are, you need direction in some area of your life at this very moment. Whatever you are facing now, Jesus has already taken care of it. I wrote the second verse of "This I Know for Sure" as a word of encouragement for those times when you need the assurance that everything will be OK:

> When the days are cloudy
> Skies are grey with rain
> The storm will soon pass over
> And I'll remember once again
>
> There is a God in Heaven
> And I am in His plan
> He will forsake me never
> My life is in His hands
> His boundless love will lead me
> As long as time endures
> Oh, this I know
> This I know for sure

Are you persuaded that God's plan is the absolute best plan for you? Do you have faith to believe this truth without wavering? You know, God doesn't panic just because you are going through a situation that causes you to panic. You might say, "But, God, life is so hard for me right now! Don't You see me suffering? Hey, God! Are You even up there?" He responds in His still, small voice, "I know what I'm doing. I have it all planned out—plans to take care of you, not abandon you, plans to give you the future you hope for" (Jeremiah 29:11 THE MESSAGE).

Although you cannot see God, you may not feel God, and at times you may not even see much evidence of His working, you must *know* that God *is* at work. Nothing can obstruct God's plan. Not people. Not things. Not even hell itself can keep God's great plan for you from coming to pass. The psalmist David cried out:

> The LORD is my rock, my fortress, my Savior.
> My God is my rock.
>   I can run to him for safety.
> He is my shield and my saving strength,
>   my defender and my place of safety. (2 Samuel 22:2-3 NCV)

Reread those verses, more slowly this time, and take a moment to break them down. God is your rock; He is your fortress (protection); He is your Savior; He is your hiding place; He is your shield; He is your saving strength; He is your defender; He is your place of safety. Who wouldn't serve a God like that?

STAY ON COURSE

God's plan is flawless and precise from beginning to end. The hope you have in Christ gives you every reason to hope for the best. Believers can always stay the course by looking at life through the eyes of hope. We don't give up because we experience pain and loss. No, we trust God and believe things will get better. That is God's plan:

> This is what the LORD Almighty, the God of Israel, says to all those I carried into exile from Jerusalem to Babylon: "Build houses and settle down; plant gardens and eat what they produce. Marry and have sons and daughters; find wives for your sons and give your daughters in marriage so that they too may have sons and daughters. Increase in

number there; do not decrease. Also, seek the peace and prosperity of the city to which I have carried you into exile. Pray to the LORD for it, because if it prospers, you too will prosper." (Jeremiah 29:4-7 NIV)

The Lord told His people not to trust in their own strength but to trust Him for everything. As they continued with the business of living, they saw God meeting all their daily needs, and their hope began to rise. Remember this: as long as you have life and breath, no matter how tough the situation may seem, you must *always* hope for the best. You see, hope is not wishing on a star or waiting for a chance. Sometimes living in hope means doing the hard thing. Hope is a confident expectation of good. Hope is a person, and that person is Jesus. No matter how hard things get, believers in Jesus must always hold on to hope. Hope is the belief that the best is yet to come.

Because of the hope we have in Christ, we should never hear of a hopeless Christian. That, my friend, is an oxymoron. The words *hopeless* and *Christian* are two contradictory terms. You have every reason to hope in Christ! You might say, "But, Babbie, the bottom has dropped out of the economy, and I've got way too much month and not enough money." Listen, dear one. Don't stand on what your paycheck says. Stand on what the Apostle Paul said in Philippians 4:19: "My God shall supply all your need according to his riches in glory by Christ Jesus." Your reply might be, "But, Babbie, I listen to the news every day. The housing market has bottomed out. I just got laid off from my job. It's all so discouraging. Sometimes I feel like giving up." Let me challenge you again not to be distracted by what you see or feel. Here's a reminder from Psalm 71:14, to focus on what you know for sure: "I will always have hope / and will praise you more and more" (NCV). The word of God tells us that there is no such thing as a hopeless situation.

There is no hopeless marriage, no hopeless financial problem, no hopeless health diagnosis. You can believe this truth from Romans 8:28 for certain, placing emphasis on the word *know*: "We *know* that all things work together for good to them that love God, to them who are the called according to his purpose" (emphasis mine).

TRUST GOD TO LEAD

Life is truly an adventure when you walk with the Lord. As I look back over the course of my life and ministry, I find that the greatest challenges were really disguised as some of the greatest opportunities for adventure, and those adventures gave God latitude to work in my life.

Back in 1986, I was invited to sing for the Governor's Prayer Breakfast here in the state of Georgia. Mr. Cliff Barrows of the Billy Graham Association was the keynote speaker for the early morning event. I was instructed to sing two songs. I had it all worked out in my mind. First, I planned to sing one of my favorite hymns, "Great Is Thy Faithfulness," from the piano. Then I envisioned a segue from the piano to center stage, during what I had hoped would be wild and thunderous applause, to sing another song from there.

On the day of the prayer breakfast, the room was packed with people, many who would leave the event and head straight to work. I was introduced to sing while people were still eating. As I concluded my first selection, I heard light applause. But what I heard more were the clinking of silverware, the clanging of dishes, and the humming of conversation around the huge breakfast tables. The audience, mostly consisting of businesspeople, continued eating. There was no wild and thunderous applause. The emcee, assuming I was finished, rushed to the podium, continuing with the program. So there was no second selection. Disappointed, I went back to my seat. To add insult to injury, my breakfast had grown cold, so I passed my uneaten breakfast to the server as he collected dishes.

Although things hadn't turned out as I had hoped, at least I could breathe a sigh of relief that the moment of performing was behind me. Mr. Barrows was introduced, and he stepped to the podium. In his introductory remarks, I never expected to hear him say these words: " 'Great Is Thy Faithfulness' is one of my favorite hymns. I'd like to extend an invitation to Mrs. Mason to be our special music guest at our upcoming Billy Graham Crusade in Tallahassee, Florida."

I couldn't believe what I was hearing. Even the audience showed their support for one of their local residents who would have such a grand opportunity. That invitation, almost twenty years ago, has led to wonderful opportunities to sing in domestic and international crusades with the Graham Association and other related events. You see, although you may not know how it's going to work out, and it may seem that no one is pulling for you, don't forget that God is on your side. And if God is for you, who can be against you (Romans 8:31)?

Even your disappointments can have happy endings when you rely on God's plan. He can use apparent setbacks to catapult you into your next season of possibility. I'm a witness to that fact. You may not always take the conventional route. There is nothing typical about the way God works, but you'll always end up at the right destination, even when you're not always sure how you'll get there or where you'll end up. This I know for sure: as you release your choke hold on the steering wheel, God promises to guide you every mile of the way.

THE ONE TRUE VOICE

The other day I asked my smartphone for directions.

"Please give me directions to Augusta, Georgia," I said.

The voice from the phone spoke with confidence: "I don't have directions to Thomas Gusta Sawyer."

I had to laugh. You see, my friend, you can seek directions from all kinds of sources. However, you may or may not get the answer you need because any source but the Lord may prove unreliable. But God *always* has the correct answer. You can depend on that. You may not know every detail. That's OK. Leave the details to a great big God who holds the future in His hands. He promises to give you reliable direction. *Every time!* Your part is to listen to His familiar voice and let Him lead you.

CHAPTER 5

DEMONSTRATING GOD'S CHARACTER

Heaven and earth shall pass away:
but my words shall not pass away.
—Luke 21:33

Every year I have the opportunity to speak to students in colleges and universities across the country. Often I have the privilege to share my knowledge and experiences as a song-writer. Other times I am able to teach students concerning the attributes and character of the Christian recording artist and worship leader. Twice annually I have the honor of teaching up-and-coming singers and songwriters at an event that

Charles and I host called the Inner Circle. Many of these students and attendees consider me an instructor, even a mentor, and I'm humbled to think that some might be following in my footsteps or that others may follow my advice strictly because I suggested it.

Trust me, I don't take the responsibility lightly. If you've ever taught students, you know that they observe not only what you say but also how you say it. In other words, people are taking notes on you. When I teach students, I often think of these words of Ralph Waldo Emerson: "Character is higher than intellect. . . . A great soul will be strong to live, as well as strong to think."[1] I also consider Psalm 19:14 the prayer of my heart: "Let the words of my mouth and the meditation of my heart, be acceptable in thy sight, O LORD, my strength and my redeemer."

Once, while lecturing at a well-known Christian university, I was sharing how a song I had written in the early 1990s, "With All My Heart," was inspired. I told the class that one perfectly beautiful spring Saturday I was driving back home from Macon to Atlanta after singing in a wedding. The wild azaleas, dogwood trees, and tulips were in full bloom. I turned off my car radio to enjoy the scenery in peace. Not long after, the words began to come to me:

> With all my heart
> I want to love You, Lord
> And live my life
> Each day to know You more
> All that is in me,
> Is Yours completely
> I'll serve You only
> With all my heart[2]

After the class was over, a beautiful Korean student approached me. She told me that, as a young girl growing up in Korea, she had sung "With All My Heart" every Sunday in her church as the benediction. She stood before me and, in a beautiful soprano voice, sang the words to the song in the language of her birth. I was so humbled by her words, I was moved to tears. The weight of that young lady's simple but profound words reminded me that people read our lives like an open book long before they may even meet us. It's true. What we do speaks louder than what we say.

CHARACTER AND TRUTH

It's sobering to think about, but people are forming impressions of us, whether we realize it or not. Have you ever said of someone, "She's such a nice person! I enjoy being around her"? Or what about this statement: "I can't put my finger on it, but there's something about that guy that concerns me"? You can learn much about a person's character by how she treats you and interacts with others. The same can be said of us—true character is often revealed in the way we encounter other people.

The word *character* describes an individual's essential attributes or moral excellence. *Character* means having qualities that distinguish you from others. Your complex mental and ethical traits set you apart from anyone else on the planet. Your character lies at the base of your attitude and personality and describes the kind of person you really are. Every one of us has inherent character traits, for good or for bad. You are to be commended if your character is described as kind, patient, generous, faithful, honest, and loyal. And you know you've got work to do if you've ever been described as jealous, manipulative, contentious, conceited, or argumentative.

Face it. For the most part, we all possess some good and some not-so-good character traits. We need to know Jesus because without the power of Christ in our lives, our character can be desperately flawed. But with the help of Jesus, we can embrace His truth and walk it out on a daily basis.

First, we must allow our character to be shaped by truth. People may have varying definitions of what the word *truth* means, but truth is defined by God's word. Truth is firm, faithful, and factual; it is absolute, not obsolete. Truth is not subjective. It is not based on opinion. It is not biased, prejudiced, or outdated. Truth is objective. It is impartial, fair, just, and based on what God has said. God is truth, and truth is defined by His character alone. Jesus said, "Heaven and earth shall pass away: but my words shall not pass away" (Luke 21:33). God has given us the Bible, His words, as our owner's manual for truth. It is our textbook for living and defining truth. God has also given us His Holy Spirit to lead and guide us into all truth. When everything else fades away, truth will be left standing.

SINCERITY IN ACTION

The story goes that a pastor of a large church in Texas was in a hurry after finishing some work at the church office. He had to run to the mall to buy a few items, go to his daughter's school to pick her up, take her home, run to a deacons' meeting, and then spend time that evening in counseling sessions. Once he was in the mall, he saw a sign on the music store window that said, "2 CDs for $9.99." He loved music so much he decided that he'd have to take advantage of the sale. He went inside and picked up two CDs he really wanted. Then he went to the register to pay for them. He passed his money to the clerk, all the time talking to everyone around him, as pastors are known to do. He picked up his purchase and his change and headed for the parking lot.

When he tossed the bag on the front seat of the car, he noticed that the clerk had charged him only $1.99 instead of $9.99 for the CDs. His first thought was that he didn't have time to go back into the mall to settle the issue with the music store clerk. But a still, small voice kept saying, "You don't have time *not* to." So he went back into the store, stood in line again, and waited his turn to speak with the clerk.

"Look, I'm in a bit of a hurry, but you made a mistake," he said. "The sign says, '2 CDs for $9.99,' but you only charged me $1.99. I owe you some money, and I'd appreciate it if you'd make the correction."

"Sir, I didn't make a mistake," she said.

"Yes, you did. There is the sign, and here is my receipt."

"No, sir, I didn't make a mistake."

"What do you mean?"

She paused a minute. "Can I tell you the rest of my story, please? For seventeen years I've not attended any church at all. Recently, however, my life has been falling apart at the seams, and I've felt a need to get back in church. I looked around for a church that was close to my home. I found the name of a church. I went there this past Sunday, slipped into the back, and sat on the last row. That day the pastor was speaking on integrity. It just so happened that it was your church I attended. So when I saw you in my line, I wondered if this was something you simply preached on Sunday or if it was something you actually lived on Monday. So I was determined to find out.

"Sir, I don't even know all the right questions to ask. But I know that whatever it is you have, I need."

Then she began to cry. The store manager, who happened to be a Christian, stepped in, took over the register, and dismissed her to speak with the pastor. The pastor shared the love of Christ with the store clerk, and she invited Jesus to be her Lord and Savior.

Do you think she would have stepped foot in a church again if the pastor had not come back into the store? Praise God, that preacher lived the life he preached about!

What a powerful testimony! Are you helping or hindering the cause of Christ by your attitudes and actions? Has someone you know come to know the Lord because of your Christlike character? Or has someone questioned the validity of your faith because of your character? *Merriam-Webster's Dictionary* defines *truth* as "sincerity in action." You might ask, "So, Babbie, is it *really* possible for a person to live a life that exemplifies truth and godly character?" Here is a noteworthy saying I've been sharing in more recent years: "Your walk talks and your talk talks. But your walk talks louder than your talk talks." That catchy but true statement inspired a song I wrote with a great songwriter, Rodney Griffin of Greater Vision, one of southern gospel music's most beloved quartets. The message is powerful:

What did you do today, to give your love away
To a lost and hurting soul?
Did you lend a hand, to a fellow man
And help him on down the road?
When you illuminate, you chase the dark away
So let your little light shine
When we follow through, in what we say and do
The Father will be glorified

You know your walk talks, and your talk talks
But your walk talks louder than your talk talks
Your behavior toward your neighbor
Tells really how you feel about the Savior

When you exemplify and shine the light of Christ
You know the number in the kingdom will be multiplied
Yes, your walk talks, and your talk talks
But your walk talks louder than your talk talks[3]

CONFORMING TO GOD'S WORD

It is possible to live in this world without conforming to it. The Apostle Paul wrote,

> I beseech you therefore, brethren, by the mercies of God, that ye present your bodies a living sacrifice, holy, acceptable unto God, which is your reasonable service. And be not conformed to this world: but be ye transformed by the renewing of your mind, that ye may prove what is that good, and acceptable, and perfect, will of God. (Romans 12:1-2)

Listen to the way *THE MESSAGE* states this powerful passage:

> Here's what I want you to do, God helping you: Take your everyday, ordinary life—your sleeping, eating, going-to-work, and walking-around life—and place it before God as an offering. Embracing what God does for you is the best thing you can do for him. Don't become so well-adjusted to your culture that you fit into it without even thinking. Instead, fix your attention on God. You'll be changed from the inside out. Readily recognize what he wants from you, and quickly respond to it. Unlike the culture around you, always dragging you down to its level of immaturity, God brings the best out of you, develops well-formed maturity in you.

With God's help we can walk according to His precepts even when those around us are not. Do you sometimes feel the pressure of the world's values trying to squeeze you into its mold? The passage above in Romans 12 tells us, even though we feel the pressure, we don't have to cave in to it. If we don't guard against them, worldly thinking and behavior will creep into our conversations and behaviors in subtle ways. Does any of this sound familiar?

Popular culture says, "It's not your fault."

Popular thinking says, "No one will ever know."

Popular psychology says, "You can't help it. It's your parents' fault."

Popular music says, "It's your thing. You can do what you want to do."

Popular opinion says, "If it feels good, do it."

Popular friends say, "It's all good. Everybody else is doing it."

Popular counsel says, "Find a way to cope with it."

Popular preaching says, "God helps those who help themselves."

Popular reasoning says, "Although it doesn't belong to me, I'll still take it. I deserve it."

Every day, you are more than likely being bombarded with worldly mind-sets that have the potential to compromise godly character. But God enables us to walk like Jesus and talk like Jesus when others are behaving as the world. Have you ever seen a toddler stack building blocks? Because he is immature, his tower of blocks will soon take a tumble. Don't allow your spiritual walk to resemble that. God wants us to abandon immature ways of thinking and grow in the knowledge of Christ. When we do this, amazing things will happen.

Ephesians 4:14 reassures us that "we will no longer be infants, tossed back and forth by the waves, and blown here and there by every wind of teaching and by the cunning and craftiness of people in their deceitful scheming" (NIV).

Think about this for a moment. If you are not progressing in your Christian growth, you are digressing. What is the one thing that demands your time and attention? Whatever it is, it will soon demand your full devotion. Allow truth to be the "one thing" that keeps your heart devoted to God. His word says, "You shall know the truth, and the truth shall make you free" (John 8:32 NKJV™).

CHARACTER ON DISPLAY

No one is perfect. We will often miss the mark. But when we do make a wrong decision, God is always there to help us. No one knows that better than I do. Not long ago, mechanical problems caused the flight I was on to be canceled, causing huge delays while the airline rerouted passengers. I was scheduled to sing that evening in Dallas, Texas, and I didn't have a moment to lose. Long, slow-moving lines, lots of impatient people, and stressed-out airline agents didn't help matters any.

By the time I stepped up to the counter, I was anxious about making it to Dallas on time. I was concerned, wondering whether my luggage would make the flight, and perturbed because the airline didn't have enough agents at the counter. It seemed the line I was in, the line for frequent fliers, was moving much slower than the others. I was ready to give the agent a piece of my mind.

The agent smiled and said, "Hi, Babbie Mason! I *love* your music!" Under my breath, I quickly begged God's forgiveness and thanked Him for intercepting my missteps and any potential damage I might've done to the kingdom of God. Thank God, He is willing to help us in our time of weakness. He is slow to anger and quick to forgive (Psalm 103:8).

Have you ever considered how your character could reflect God's kingdom here on earth? God knows the motives and intents of our hearts. He punishes sin, but He rewards those who honor His word: "The upright shall dwell in the land, and the men of integrity, blameless *and* complete [in God's sight], shall remain in it; but the wicked shall be cut off from the earth, and the treacherous shall be rooted out of it" (Proverbs 2:21-22 AMP).

The story goes that a preacher asked his congregation to read the second chapter of the book of Jude by the following Sunday. The next Sunday, the minister asked from the pulpit how many had read the passage. A large number of congregants raised their hands.

"There is only one chapter in the book of Jude," said the minister. "This morning, I am speaking on truth and character."

Always remember that people may doubt what you say, but they will always believe what you do. God is searching for people He can count on to do both: speak the truth, then back it up with actions that please Him. This is the best way we can honor God and His word and ultimately carry out His plan. Your character speaks volumes. Others are taking notes on you. What does your character say about you? Does your life demonstrate to others that you are a child of God who honors the truth of His word? Here is an old thought to hide in your heart: "the only Jesus some people may see is the Jesus they see in you and in me."

CHAPTER 6
_____

_____

PURSUING GOD'S PURPOSE
_____

Look carefully then how you walk!
Live purposefully and worthily and accurately,
not as the unwise and witless, but as wise
(sensible, intelligent people).
—_Ephesians 5:15 AMP_

E verything about your life is significant. No matter how unremarkable or run-of-the-mill it may seem, everything about you is wrapped up in God's purpose. There is not a single moment left to chance. God desires that you live your life on purpose—with a purpose and for a purpose. I hope you are beginning to see that if you are not fulfilling God's purpose for your life, you haven't begun to live. You will never achieve your dreams and goals apart from God's plan for you. How do we know this? We need only look at the life of Christ, the only One capable of fulfilling His ordained purpose to the letter.

When He was here on earth, Jesus knew it was vital to live out His Father's specific plan. Just before He went to the cross, Jesus prayed to His Father concerning the work He had completed up to that moment: "Having finished the work you gave me to do, I brought you glory on earth" (John 17:4 NCV). What a powerful proclamation! Jesus' only desire was to do the will of His Father and bring Him glory. Can you say the same? Have you earnestly asked God to help you discover His beautiful design for your life with the intention of bringing Him glory?

Jesus spent the better part of the last three years of His life teaching His disciples how to live a life that is glorifying to God. Jesus didn't just tell them; He showed them how to walk out God's purpose in the earth. Jesus taught the disciples how to grow spiritually by patterning their lives after Him. That's *discipleship*. He taught them to love God and develop intimacy with Him. That's *worship*. Then He taught them how to love others and to serve others with humility. That's *relationship*. Those three qualities bring blessing to our lives, encouragement to others, and glory to God.

SEIZING EVERY OPPORTUNITY

I am often greatly encouraged by how God uses my husband, Charles, to show me what discipleship, worship, and relationship actually look like when lived out.

One Sunday morning, Charles and I were flying home from Florida, where I had been in a concert the night before. We'd only gotten a few hours of sleep before we had to rise way before dawn to catch an early morning flight to Atlanta. But I really didn't mind. I was excited because we'd be able to get to church later that morning. I was looking forward to sitting in my favorite seat and enjoying the music and the sermon after being away for several Sundays in a row. I was very happy when the plane landed at Atlanta's airport right on time.

Although we didn't have time to waste, everything was running like clockwork. We got our luggage in a reasonable time. We picked up our truck from the satellite parking lot and headed to the expressway. At an exit near the church, Charles noticed that the truck's fuel tank was near empty so we stopped to refuel. We had about twenty minutes to spare before the worship service was scheduled to begin, so we'd still have to hurry to find a parking spot and arrive in time to find seats close to the front of the sanctuary. Although I'd probably not be able to sit in my favorite seat, I wanted to get as close to the front as I could. After being away for so long, I didn't want to miss a single word.

Charles pumped the gas and went inside to pay. On the way out, he paused a moment as he noticed two young fellows whose car was in deep distress. One of them pushed the powerless vehicle with all his might while the other tried desperately to steer it to a parking spot. Charles stepped in behind their car and helped push it. After the car came to a stop, Charles nodded his head to their thanks and headed back to the truck we were in. I admired my husband's generous spirit. *It is nice of him to stop and help those young guys,* I thought, *but it is time to get to church.* As Charles opened the door to the driver's side, he glanced back to see the two young men struggling to raise the hood of their car. It was obvious they didn't know the difference between a headlight and a tailpipe.

Without missing a beat, Charles hopped into our truck, closed the door, and drove over to lend a hand. I looked at the clock on the truck's dashboard. Worship service would be starting in a few minutes. All Charles had to do was make a quick determination that the car was beyond his ability to fix it, and we could be on our way, I was sure. One look at their car made it obvious it didn't need repair. It needed a resurrection!

After closer inspection, Charles determined there was something he could do to help, and he went right to it. I rolled down the window just enough to keep the heat in and the chilly spring wind out. I could hear the conversation between Charles and the young travelers. Listening closely, I could hear their distinctive accents, and I recognized those beautiful angular features. I knew Charles recognized them. I could tell he, too, was intrigued by these two strangers, who appeared to be from Africa. Having visited Kenya, Uganda, and South Africa, Charles and I have had the opportunity to help dig wells and build churches, schools, and medical clinics in these countries. The friendships we have established there are lifelong.

Finally I heard Charles say something about the battery. The young men knew they were in good hands as they stepped back to lean against the building, keeping their hands warm in their pockets. They could tell that my husband knew what he was doing, and they were not about to interrupt him. Like a well-trained surgeon, Charles made his diagnosis and went to work on their ailing vehicle. Charles, a Johnny-on-the-spot Vietnam veteran who was born in the rural South, can find a solution for just about any emergency. With Charles in charge, the young men were fortunate indeed.

On the other hand, I sat stewing in the truck. I realized there was no way we'd make it to church on time. Gone was my opportunity to hear wonderful music. Gone was my opportunity to hear an inspired sermon. Gone was my chance to see my friends. I wouldn't have another opportunity to be at our home church to worship for several more weeks. Just then I heard Charles instruct one of the guys to hop in and start the car. Without hesitation, one fellow climbed behind the wheel. The car's motor coughed and sputtered a few times but eventually turned over. With a couple ferocious pats on the accelerator, the car began to clear its throat.

I glanced over at the young man behind the wheel. His eyes caught mine as he smiled with pure delight. It was then I saw something I hadn't seen before. I wondered about these young men. How did they get to the United States? Where were their parents? Were they here or back in Africa? What about their mothers? Could a mother be somewhere praying that very moment that when her son was stranded somewhere along the side of the road, some kind and caring person would come along to help? Maybe their parents had been victims of a violent civil war. Could these young men, between the ages of my own two sons, be refugees *and* orphans? Tears welled up in my eyes and compassion gripped my heart as I imagined what the stories of these two might be. I've been to Africa enough times to know that whatever the story was, it was probably mingled with pain and loss.

I watched as my husband finished working on their car and told them what part they needed. He spoke to them like a father. They listened like sons. With care and compassion, Charles did as Jesus would do. I watched this powerful scene being played out before me, and I bowed my head under conviction and whispered a prayer of forgiveness to God. Then I whispered a prayer of thanks for a man like Charles, the good Samaritan, who was kind and willing to help two strangers in trouble. Can you imagine the encouragement they received that day from being recipients of Charles's servant heart?

I realized, right then and there, that I *had* been to church. I had witnessed a great sermon, complete with illustrations. I had prayed a heartfelt prayer and responded to the Lord's invitation. I even sang a song while Charles gave the two a few instructions. My heart was full, as full as it has been after many worship services. Charles was able to put discipleship, worship, and relationship on display in living color.

HOW ARE YOU GROWING?

If Jesus were to call you in for an evaluation of the quality of your work and the attitude with which you carried it out, what do you think His response would be?

1. "Well done, good and faithful servant."
2. "Your work could use some improvement."
3. "When will you get started?"

Now hear this: God is more interested in *who* you are than in *what* you do. He wants you to live out your purpose while helping others to discover theirs. This living-out process of following after Christ, learning what He did and how He did it, then doing what Christ would do is called discipleship.

Are you a disciple of Christ? Can others tell whose side

you're on? Your Christlike life is your mark of discipleship. Living a life that brings glory to Christ is the quality that sets you apart from the world. This doesn't mean that you won't make mistakes. It means that you look to Jesus to establish the pattern for how you'll live your life. When we stand before God, He will not ask us whether we were good people. He will not ask us whether we were good members of the Baptist church, the Methodist church, or some other denomination. All that will matter is whether we followed Christ. The true mark of discipleship is that you are growing up and maturing into the person God has designed you to become.

HOW'S YOUR WORSHIP?

A songwriter friend, Tony Sutherland, wrote a great book called *Graceworks*. In it, he talks about real worship:

> So often we focus on the *way* we worship rather than on the *One* we worship. In other words, the emphasis is on the mechanics of worship rather than on the Lord of our worship. It is sad to say but many times we give more attention to creativity than we do the Creator! We're not supposed to worship the worship! Jesus alone is the object of our fondest affection! When Jesus (the person of grace) is exalted, people from every walk of life will respond to His unconditional love and surrender to His uncontested Lordship (John 12:32).[1]

Worship is honoring God with your life. You can never repay Jesus for all that He has done for you. Your good works can't repay Him. Church attendance can't repay Him. On your best day, your best still falls short. But Jesus fixed all that. He paid it all, once and for all! A life of worship focuses on what Christ has already done at the cross, not on what you have done. In response, the heart that worships produces a life of obedience, and obedience is the mark of a true disciple. Worship is your response for all that Christ has done for you.

The world measures us by our successes and accomplishments, while God measures us by our faithfulness and obedience. Consider Peter, one of Christ's most devoted disciples. Although he walked with Jesus every day for three years, Peter was a man with many shortcomings. In the eyes of the world, some might consider Peter a failure. He attempted to walk on water, but he sank (Matthew 14:28-33). Peter showed how impulsive he was when he hastily cut off a soldier's ear in the garden of Gethsemane during Jesus' arrest (John 18:10). Peter denied Jesus three times (Matthew 26:69-75). Peter was found to be a hypocrite (Galatians 2:11-14). But was Peter a failure? Absolutely not. Why? Because even when he fell short, Jesus was there to fully restore him. The same is true for us. Even in the midst of life's greatest failures, Jesus invites us into His presence to enjoy intimate friendship with Him.

The world is concerned about religion while Jesus is concerned about relationship. You can't build a relationship with Jesus without taking time to be connected to Him. Religious people care more about possessions and status than the condition of the heart. But your position in life doesn't matter to Jesus; He is looking for a heart of devotion. Are you connected to Jesus, enjoying intimate moments with Him on a daily basis? If you need help getting started, practice the following routine each day:

- Give God the opportunity to say something to you daily through the study of His word (Acts 17:11). Read at least one chapter of the Bible daily. By reading four chapters daily, you will read through the whole Bible in a year.

- Take the opportunity to say something to God daily through devotion and prayer (1 Thessalonians 5:16-17).
- Take the opportunity to say something for God daily (2 Timothy 4:2). Share your salvation story with a friend, or offer a word of encouragement to someone who is discouraged (Ephesians 4:32).
- Take the opportunity to do something for God daily. Look for ways you can give God glory by being a blessing to others (Colossians 3:17).

HOW'S YOUR SERVE?

God is not as concerned about your ability as He is about your availability. Worldly people seek to be served; godly people seek to serve. The person behind the scenes is just as important as the one in the spotlight on center stage. What matters most is that your life is dedicated to serving Christ and giving Him glory with your God-given gifts and talents. In what area has God assigned you to serve? Are you being faithful to that call no matter what?

When the Italian city of Pompeii was destroyed by the volcanic eruption of Mount Vesuvius in AD 79, many people were buried alive by the hot lava and were later found preserved in its aftermath. Some were found in the streets, attempting to flee the city. Some were in deep vaults, hoping to find security there. Some were discovered in lofty chambers high above ground, hoping to escape the destructive lava. Where could the Roman sentinel be found? He was found standing at the city gate, at his post of duty, where his captain had placed him. Still armed with his weapon, he stood there while the heavens rained fire and ash; he stood there while the earth quaked violently beneath him; he stood there as lava and pumice pummeled him. He was found, almost two thousand years later, at his post of duty.

Each of us has a post of duty where Jesus, our Captain, has placed us. Can you be found at your post of duty, relentlessly serving Jesus today?

LIVING FOR HIM

Your walk talks louder than your talk. So what is your walk saying about you? Is it saying, "I'm determined to get ahead no matter what it takes"? Is your walk saying something like, "I'm tired of waiting on God. I'm going to do things my way"?

If you are looking to others rather than to Jesus for your answers, dear friend, I'm here to tell you that you'll be drawing from an empty well. Anything that is isolated and disconnected from its life source will eventually die. So let me encourage you to make up your mind that you're not just going to live for "something" but that you'll live for someone—Christ. Make this your declaration today: "I am crucified with Christ: nevertheless I live; yet not I, but Christ liveth in me: and the life which I now live in the flesh I live by the faith of the Son of God, who loved me, and gave himself for me" (Galatians 2:20).

This I know for sure: you were born on purpose, with a purpose, and for a purpose. The moment you make this discovery is the very moment you really will begin to live.

PART THREE

THERE IS A GOD IN HEAVEN
AND I AM IN HIS PLAN

He will forsake me never

My life is in His hands
His boundless love will lead me
As long as time endures
Oh, this I know
This I know for sure

Come, ye disconsolate, where'er ye languish,
come to the mercy seat, fervently kneel.
Here bring your wounded hearts, here tell your anguish;
earth has no sorrow that heaven cannot heal.

Joy of the desolate, light of the straying,
hope of the penitent, fadeless and pure!
Here speaks the Comforter, tenderly saying,
"Earth has no sorrow that heaven cannot cure."

Here see the bread of life; see waters flowing
forth from the throne of God, pure from above.
Come to the feast of love; come, ever knowing
earth has no sorrow but heaven can remove.

—Thomas Moore, Thomas Hastings[1]

CHAPTER 7
_____

_____
IN THE MEAN TIMES
_____

While they were sailing, he fell asleep. Gale-force winds swept down on
the lake. The boat was filling up with water and they were in danger. So
they went and woke Jesus, shouting, "Master, Master, we're going to
drown!" But he got up and gave orders to the wind and the violent waves.
The storm died down and it was calm.
—Luke 8:23-24 CEB

In recent years we have witnessed the devastation that in-
tense weather-related storms can cause. In 2005, Hurricane
Katrina hit the US Gulf coast, and in 2012 we saw the deadly
effects of Superstorm Sandy, which ravaged the Caribbean,

the mid-Atlantic, and the northeastern United States. Even here in the state of Georgia, we have seen violent tornadoes and floods destroy entire communities in a matter of minutes. Though storms are natural weather phenomena we've come to expect, even anticipate, the damage that storms leave behind can take years to rebuild and cost billions of dollars to clean up.

Personal storms are also a reality. You know as well as I do how storms—in the form of an unexpected diagnosis from a doctor, the foreclosure of a home, the death of a loved one, an assault on a marriage—can bear down on us. Any one of these events can bring the best of us to our knees. Whatever the circumstances, when a storm wreaks havoc in your life, there is no insurance company or government agency competent enough to fix the fallout from the wreckage. But take heart, my friend. You do have a safe place to run for shelter.

Jesus is a refuge from every storm. Because Jesus loves you, He will never leave you to face the storm alone. He knows how to speak peace to the torrential winds and waves that dash against you.

BUILDING STRONG

My mother, a very wise and resilient woman, has always taken stormy weather in stride. Years ago, she gave me wise counsel concerning storms: "You're either in a storm, coming out of a storm, or headed for another storm. Rain or shine, the weather doesn't bother me. We're going to have weather whether we like it or not." My mother is right. Storms in our atmosphere and in our lives are inevitable. It doesn't matter how old you are, where you were born, or your income bracket;

if you live on this planet you're going to encounter mean times. Storms will blow through your life.

You know how it is. One minute, everything is fine, and you are cruising through life under sunny skies. The next thing you know, without warning, the skies turn black and the bottom drops out. But here is what I know for sure: every storm I've been in lasted only a season. The storm didn't come to stay. The storm came to pass.

About ten years ago, Charles and I moved from the bustling city to a quiet spot in the country. There, we built our new home from the ground up. When it came to building, I could tell you just the kind of house I wanted. I knew the square footage, style, color scheme, size of the kitchen, and the number of bedrooms I wanted. What I didn't talk much about was the foundation. There's nothing pretty about a deep hole hewn out of the ground. There's nothing fashionable about concrete walls and steel rods in sturdy construction. But the foundation is the most important part of our home. The foundation bears the weight of our entire house, supporting floors, furniture, appliances, family, guests, and the grand piano my dad gave me when Charles and I got married.

Fortunately God tells us how to build strong foundations for our lives, foundations that will support us through the approaching storms. In the book of Matthew, Jesus teaches us a lesson on how to build a home, a relationship, a business, and a family. Who would know better than a master builder not just how to stormproof your house but how to stormproof your life? Read His words:

> Everyone who hears these words of Mine and acts on them, may be compared to a wise man who built his house on the rock. And the rain fell, and the floods came, and the winds blew and slammed against

that house; and yet it did not fall, for it had been founded on the rock. Everyone who hears these words of Mine and does not act on them will be like a foolish man who built his house on the sand. The rain fell, and the floods came, and the winds blew and slammed against that house; and it fell—and great was its fall. (Matthew 7:24-27 NASB)

At the time Jesus spoke this building analogy, He was concluding His famous Sermon on the Mount, beginning in Matthew 5. Jesus told the huge gathering of people listening that day: "Everyone who hears these words of Mine and acts on them, may be compared to a wise man who built his house on the rock." Jesus' words were not just for the select few who heard Him that day. He knew that tough times would affect everyone. And Jesus knew that all kinds of people search for truth, for answers to the dilemmas they face. People like you and I need a firm place to stand when the gale-force winds of life threaten everything that isn't nailed down. And as Jesus told us, the only thing that will allow us to stand against the storms of life is firmly believing His word.

STANDING STRONG

My husband, Charles, and I have been through some pretty mean times in recent years. During the course of our marriage, we have felt the brunt of some of life's most turbulent storms. One morning in March 2010, Charles awakened early complaining that he couldn't see at all out of his right eye! Immediately, we rushed to the ophthalmologist's office for an emergency appointment. The doctor told Charles that he had suffered a stroke in his eye. With the doctor's grim diagnosis came a more dismal prognosis.

The doctor said to Charles, "You've suffered a stroke in your right eye. Your eye is gone, and you will be blind in that eye for the rest of your life. You may as well kiss that eye good-bye."

With each word from the doctor's mouth, I felt as if I was being punched in the pit of my stomach. The weight of his forecast caused my heart to sink into a pit of despair. I could feel the ominous storm clouds of fear and panic sweep into the room.

Then the doctor said something that made my spirit stand at attention: "Apart from a miracle, you will never see out of that eye again."

When I heard the word *miracle*, it was as if the clouds rolled back and hope shined a light onto a hopeless situation. I opened my mouth and defied his pronouncement: "We're going to allow God to have the last word on that! Beginning now, that's what we are going to believe God for—a miracle!"

Charles was admitted to intensive care at the nearby hospital. While he was being examined, I got on the phone and called friends and family and asked them to pray for the miracle we were believing God could perform. Within twenty-four hours, Charles's vision began to return! Even over recent months, he is experiencing changes and improvement in his vision, though it is not yet 100 percent. But, praise God, he's not blind! And we are still believing God will finish the work He started.

Are you experiencing a storm in your life right now? Is someone you love going through a trying situation? Psalm 107 tells of people who were caught in a vicious storm on the open seas. In the midst of the storm the passengers' courage seemed to melt away. But the miraculous happened when

> they cried out to the LORD in their trouble,
> and he brought them out of their distress.

He stilled the storm to a whisper;
   and the waves of the seas were hushed.
They were glad when it grew calm,
   and he guided them to their desired haven. (Psalm 107:28-30 NIV)

You see, my friend, when life's violent winds assault your family, your marriage, or your home, don't back down. Call out to your trustworthy God. He has never failed, and He will not begin with you! In the way only He can, He will give you the strength you need at the precise moment you need it, and you will find yourself believing God for the impossible. Allow God to have the last word in your situation, and see the miraculous things God will do!

A FAULTY FOUNDATION

Have you ever built a sand castle at the beach? Jesus makes the reference that building your life without a strong foundation is just like that. Get this picture in your mind. It's a beautiful day at the beach, and you spend hours building an impressive and creative sand castle. It looks amazing, glistening in the afternoon sun. But you soon learn that it doesn't take much to level a sand castle. The tidewaters come rolling in, an afternoon rain shower comes pouring down, and that sand castle, as pretty as it is, has nothing to stand on. Gone. In no time there won't be a sign that it was ever there. Is this how you want to build your life, placing everything you love and value on nothing more than sand?

Jesus said that those who hear but don't act on God's wisdom are like the man who builds his house on the sand. Jesus sent out a warning here: when it rains, it pours, and everybody gets wet. The rain falls on the just as well as the unjust (Matthew

5:45). Sometimes the storms of life show no sign of letting up. Out of frustration, you've probably said, "If it's not one thing, it's another." Isn't that true? If it's not the house, it's the car. If it's not your finances, it's your health. If it's not your money, it's your honey. There's always some challenge to face. Jesus is well aware of how life's problems can compound, one on top of another. Notice how Jesus used the word *and* to describe the situation: "The rain fell, *and* the floods came, *and* the winds blew *and* slammed against that house; *and* it fell—*and* great was its fall" (Matthew 7:27 NASB, emphasis mine).

In both scenarios the rains came, the floods rose, and the winds blew. In both instances the winds slammed against the house. But in the case concerning the foolish man, his house fell, and the fall was *great*. The foolish builder took shortcuts to save time, effort, and money. In the end, that decision cost him dearly. He lost everything that was dear to him; his home, his family, and even his life were damaged beyond repair.

Jesus insists it is not enough to just hear His words. Anyone can do that. Religious people do that all the time. Even people who don't know Christ personally have heard His words. Scores of churchgoers warm a pew for an hour each week and listen to His word, then choose to build their lives on shaky ground. The mind-set that one can build a stable life according to the world's standards will eventually see the foundation crumble. We've all stood helplessly by, holding our proverbial breath, while the harsh winds of our times ravaged our nation's financial systems, real estate markets, education, politics, and every other man-made institution.

Jesus, the master storyteller, used the parable of the wise man and the foolish man to challenge those who are willing to listen to His words, then go to the next step and act on what they have heard. Those who act on the words of Jesus are wise, admitting in their hearts, "Jesus, I recognize Your word is truth. I trust You with my life. I believe Your word, and I'll do what You say because You know best."

Jesus revealed that it's not a matter *if* the storms will come against you but *when*. Just because you're a Christian doesn't mean you won't have difficulties. As a matter of fact, the opposite is true. As a Christian, you'll probably experience more difficulty, not because you did something wrong but because you did something right. I'm sure you know what I mean. Because believers' standards are higher, there are some things we have decided we won't do. There are places we refuse to go, with people we refuse to call friends. Your adversary, Satan, knows this too. So he will do all he can to hinder you. He wants to keep you from accomplishing great things for God.

Your enemy's mission is to put roadblocks in your way to trip you up. But if you are building your life on the wisdom of God's word, you will be wise to the ways of the enemy. You know that the stakes are high and there's too much to lose. But regardless of the forces that come against you, never forget, with God on your side, you are never, ever left defenseless.

PUTTING A STRONG FOUNDATION TO WORK

I enjoy the devotion of reading through old hymns. I am often deeply moved by these compositions, written from centuries past, by people of deep faith in Christ. Many of these men and women experienced numerous hardships, even persecution. To encourage you in your foundation building, allow me to share the words of one of the best-loved hymns, "My Hope Is Built," written by Edward Mote in 1834:

My hope is built on nothing less
than Jesus' blood and righteousness.
I dare not trust the sweetest frame,
but wholly lean on Jesus' name.

When darkness veils his lovely face,
I rest on his unchanging grace.
In every high and stormy gale,
my anchor holds within the veil.

On Christ the solid rock I stand,
All other ground is sinking sand;
All other ground is sinking sand.[1]

There are some powerful truths in this great hymn. The thought overwhelms me that two hundred years from now, it's quite possible that people may read the lyrics to any one of my songs. It's my prayer that they find the principles of truth, God's word, woven through each line, strengthening their hearts in the midst of what could be the most unsettling storms.

When we walk in God's wisdom, we are able to offer encouragement to those we meet along the way. Our lives don't always have to be overflowing with drama to learn these power-packed precepts. We just have to be ready to surrender our lives to the Lord—whatever the situation, wherever the opportunity presents itself. Earlier I told you how I missed the Lord's prompting at the airline ticket counter and how He taught me a great lesson on character. Then I told you how I missed it again when Charles stopped to help the two African travelers. The Lord taught me a great lesson on charity. I admit I tend to be a slow learner. But Pastor Jim Cymbala used powerful words in his book *Fresh Wind, Fresh Fire* that encourage me. He said, "People who have a seeking heart still make mistakes. But their reaction to rebuke and correction shows the condition of that heart."[2]

God gave me another opportunity the other day to put His love on display. I didn't miss the moment. Let me tell you about it. On yet another trip through the airport, I was in a hurry to get to my boarding gate. Of course, the gate was the last one on the concourse. With just a few minutes to spare, I was on a fast clip when I glanced to the left and saw a young female soldier, dressed in her fatigues, in line at the hot dog stand. There's something about a woman in a military uniform that always grips my heart.

The Lord prompted me to go over and buy her lunch. Even though I was in a hurry, I trusted the Lord to give me the time I needed to complete this simple mission. I lingered just long enough for the young soldier to step up to the clerk at the fast-food counter and place her order. When she did, I gingerly stepped up beside her.

I said, "Excuse me, ma'am. I hope you don't mind, but just to say thanks for your service to our country, I'd like to buy your lunch today. Would that be OK?"

She said, "Thanks, but that's not necessary."

I said, "Yeah, I know, but it's the least I can do. I'd just like to show my appreciation for the great job you're doing."

She hesitated, then said, "Well, OK. Thanks a lot."

The young soldier, probably just a year or two out of high school, placed her order for a simple hot dog with ketchup and mustard. I'd waited for such a moment to ask my next question.

"Would you like fries with that?"

The fast-food clerk, the soldier, and I laughed out loud. Her inhibitions easing, the young woman said, "No, thanks."

I saw that she was carrying a bottle of apple juice that was almost empty. "Well at least let me buy you something to wash the hot dog down," I said.

She ordered a fresh-squeezed lemonade.

While her hot dog and lemonade were being prepared, I took the time to express my thanks again for her service to our country with my promise to pray for her. We chatted, and in just a few seconds, she began to open up. She told me that she was on her way overseas and that she would be returning home in a few months. Her meal was ready in no time. She thanked me and then reached around my neck to give me a hug. I wished her Godspeed, paid for her meal, and dashed off to my gate. I was grateful that I hadn't missed it this time.

Spending a few bucks for a hot dog and lemonade was no big deal. But my heart was filled with much joy because I had been able to please the Lord by walking in His ways. It didn't stop with me either. My young soldier friend was blessed and encouraged, the restaurant clerk observed the turning of a good deed, and ultimately God received the glory.

CHRIST, THE SOLID ROCK

Don't miss it! What is *it*? *It* is the next opportunity to put the precepts of Jesus into practice. Just as Jesus spoke to the crowd that day, I believe He's speaking to your heart right now. The question is, are you listening?

If you're fortunate enough not to be in a storm right now, praise God! But may I recommend that you place a bookmark at this page so you can come back to it at a moment's notice? Don't get too comfortable. Build your hope on eternal things by shoring up your foundation with the truth of God's word. Trust me. No, let me rephrase that. Trust Jesus. For certain, another storm is headed your way, and it won't be long before it blows down your street and knocks on your front door. Remember what my mother said, "We're going to have weather whether we like it or not." Then remember what Jesus said: "Everyone who hears these words of Mine and acts on them, may be compared to a wise man who built his house on the rock."

You may be facing pretty mean times right now. Or maybe you've hunkered down in a corner, too afraid to look out the window to see whether the storm has already passed. This I know for sure: you have nothing to fear. Jesus wants you to know that He loves you, and you can always find a hiding place in Him. He will never forsake you but will keep you safe until the storm passes by.

CHAPTER 8

IN THE IN-BETWEEN TIMES

I will never leave you or abandon you.
—Hebrews 13:5 CEB

Have you ever found yourself in a situation where you had to wait for a season before the answer came? Did you ever call a customer service line only to be put on hold? Have you ever waited in the emergency room of a hospital? Are you waiting for a child to return home from college or for some improvement in your health?

I've done a good bit of waiting in my life, and I know exactly how you feel. I've waited for Christmas mornings, graduations, and a wedding day. I've waited for babies to arrive, and I've waited long into the night while sitting by the bedside of my husband when he was hospitalized. You probably feel the same way I do when it comes to waiting—I don't like it. Waiting is hard, inconvenient, and uncomfortable. It's as if time puts itself on hold while life is making up its mind what it wants to do.

We get excited when God answers our prayers quickly, don't we? You've probably prayed a prayer like this: "Answer me speedily, O LORD; / My spirit fails!" (Psalm 143:7 NKJV™). Sometimes it seems that God takes His time and we're left in limbo. Here's the good news: your waiting is not in vain. In God's economy, no time is ever wasted. God always has a plan and a purpose for the waiting.

DON'T FEAR

In the in-between times, it may seem as if God has forgotten your request. You may feel that your life is put on hold. But recall what the Lord said to Joshua, "I will not leave you nor forsake you" (Joshua 1:5 NKJV™). In the in-between times God is behind the scenes doing His best work on our behalf, and the word of God gives us specific instructions to follow while we wait on His direction. We can learn a valuable lesson as we face seasons of uncertainty by reviewing what God has done for His people in the past.

Consider the tribe of Judah. They had a great king, Jehoshaphat, who learned firsthand that God will provide just the right solution at just the right moment. (I encourage you to read the profound details of the entire chapter of 2 Chronicles 20. For now, we'll hit the highlights.)

Jehoshaphat received the news that several huge armies had banded together and were determined to destroy him and the children of Judah. With their backs against the wall and their enemies breathing down their necks, this great king knew that without God's help, they were doomed. Jehoshaphat was only human. When he learned that their enemies were gaining ground, initially he was alarmed. Who wouldn't be in that situation? But the king knew it was no time for fear. It was time for action: "Jehoshaphat feared, and set himself to seek the LORD, and proclaimed a fast throughout all Judah. And Judah gathered themselves together, to ask help of the LORD: even out of all the cities of Judah they came to seek the LORD" (2 Chronicles 20:3-4).

With the news of imminent danger, this man of God immediately called the people to fast and pray. He knew the situation was out of his hands, so he placed it into God's hands. His was a critical response. How many heartbreaks and setbacks could you have avoided if you had only sought the Lord by fasting and praying about a matter rather than taking it into your own hands?

This famous story is packed with strategic elements to help the people of God stand strong when they are waiting for the outcome. Even when the outcome is uncertain—even when you have to wait on God and trust Him every step of the way— you can know for sure He is with you while you seek Him. God instructs you not to run scared. He commands you not to be so overwhelmed and paralyzed with fear that you can't think straight. Instead, He commands you to trust and give the situation to Him. Don't be anxious or worried about uncertainties. Instead, pray about everything (Philippians 4:6-7).

Just about every book in the Bible speaks on the subject of

fear and commands us not to allow fear to control us. I've heard numerous times that the Bible mentions the words *fear not* 365 times. That's a *fear not* for every day of the year. Although this is an exaggeration, the more I study God's word, the more I find those promises. And I found an interesting pattern. Wherever those words appear, good news follows close behind. Let's look at examples:

- In 2 Chronicles 20:15 God said to the people, "Be not afraid nor dismayed by reason of this great multitude." Now read the promise: "The battle is not yours, but God's."
- In Genesis 15:1 God told Abram to "fear not." Now read the promise God gave him: "I am thy shield, and thy exceeding great reward."
- In Isaiah 41:10 God told His people to fear not, then the blessing came right behind: "I am with you. / Don't be discouraged, for I am your God. / I will strengthen you and help you. / I will hold you up with my victorious right hand" (NLT).
- In Joshua 1:9 the Lord spoke to Joshua, "Have I not commanded thee? Be strong and of a good courage; be not afraid, neither be thou dismayed." Then the powerful promise: "The LORD thy God is with thee withersoever thou goest."
- In Luke 1:30, when the angel Gabriel came to Mary, the mother of Jesus, with the news that she had been chosen to bear the Son of God, he met her with these words: "Fear not." And the promise: "Thou hast found favour with God."

- In Luke 2:10, when the angel appeared before the shepherds the night Jesus was born, the angel said, "Fear not." Now here's the promise: "Behold, I bring you good tidings of great joy, which shall be to all people."

Do you see the pattern? There are many more *fear nots* in the Bible just waiting for you to discover them. When you read them, you'll be reminded that God has commanded you never to fear, but to look instead for His powerful promises to come to pass in your life. The emotion of fear is healthy. You should have a healthy fear and respect for fire that burns out of control or for wild, dangerous animals. But the spirit of fear is not God's method of operation. The spirit of fear comes only from the enemy as a form of torment. Stand your ground and remember God's command not to fear. You might be thinking, *Well, in some situations I just can't help being fearful.* Not according to God's word! The Lord would not have given you this command if it were not possible for you to follow through with it. Paul affirmed, "God hath not given us the spirit of fear; but of power, and of love, and of a sound mind" (2 Timothy 1:7). That means, then, that it's actually possible *not* to be fearful.

DON'T FAINT

Every great leader knows he or she must have a strategy for times of war, and that begins with keeping a level head in times of imminent danger. After Jehoshaphat called a national day of prayer and fasting, he called on the forces of heaven to gird them. He didn't fall apart in the face of danger. Instead he pulled it all together. When it counted the most, he didn't emphasize his situation, reminding himself and his people how big their enemies were. He made the Lord the center of attention and reminded the entire nation how big their God is. Listen to this powerful prayer:

> Jehoshaphat stood in the congregation of Judah and Jerusalem, in the house of the LORD, before the new court, and said, O LORD God of our fathers, art not thou God in heaven? and rulest not thou over all the kingdoms of the heathen? and in thine hand is there not power and might, so that none is able to withstand thee? Art not thou our God, who didst drive out the inhabitants of this land before thy people Israel, and gavest it to the seed of Abraham thy friend for ever?
> (2 Chronicles 20:5-7)

Jehoshaphat continued, "O our God, wilt thou not judge them? for we have no might against this great company that cometh against us; neither know we what to do: but our eyes are upon thee" (v. 12).

What a powerful lesson in prayer! Did you notice that Jehoshaphat didn't rush into God's presence with a lengthy list of his personal needs, although they were critical? He didn't go to God with complaints or murmurings. First, the king proclaimed God's attributes, those qualities that tell of God's greatness. It's not that God needs to be reminded of His greatness; we are the ones who need reminding. In this prayer, the king did not recite what he was feeling about himself but rehearsed what he already knew about God. Jehoshaphat shows us that by approaching God's throne in this manner, we respond to God in faith, not out of our anxiety because of a need we currently face.

Do you have the confidence that God already knows what you need even before you ask? Do your prayers express such faith and confidence in God that whatever you ask according to His will, you believe He will do for you (Matthew 6:8)? We learn here that it is more important to honor God, who already knows our need, than to selfishly come to God with our agendas. Jehoshaphat recognized God for His ways, not just for His acts.

Does your prayer list read more like a shopping list, expressing your greed rather than your need? God is well aware that you have many needs. But never forget the One you serve. Your God is the grand need-meeter. I remember the older saints in my father's church saying from time to time: "God is rarely early. But He's never late. Now, He may not come when you want Him, but He's always on time." I can say amen to that! In between the time you pray and the time you are waiting for an answer from God, stand on your faith, believing that God will come through for you.

DON'T FIGHT

No matter the size of the war you're facing, you are to let God fight your battles. If you are beaten, bruised, and battle weary, you are fighting a battle that doesn't belong to you. You have a God who is bigger than your enemies, and He will fight for you. You do have a responsibility, however. Just as each member of a ball team has an assigned position to fill, so do you. Just as every member of a corporate staff has a specific job description, so do you. Your position is to stand and see the salvation of the Lord. Read what the Bible says in 2 Chronicles 20:14-17:

> The Spirit of the LORD [came] in the midst of the congregation; and he said, Hearken ye, all Judah, and ye inhabitants of Jerusalem, and thou king Jehoshaphat, Thus saith the LORD unto you, Be not afraid nor dismayed by reason of this great multitude; for the battle is not yours, but God's. To morrow go ye down against them: behold, they come up by the cliff of Ziz; and ye shall find them at the end of the brook, before the wilderness of Jeruel. Ye shall not need to fight in

this battle: set yourselves, stand ye still, and see the salvation of the LORD with you, O Judah and Jerusalem: fear not, nor be dismayed; to morrow go out against them: for the LORD will be with you.

Your position is important because your position determines your possession. When you stand firm on what you know, not on what you feel, you are in the position to receive from the Lord. In addition, you are clearheaded, and the Holy Spirit will show you the cunning strategies of the evil one, who wants to steal everything that is near and dear to you. I'm a witness that the Lord will teach you how to stand strong in the midst of a battle.

A few years ago, I was invited to speak at a women's conference overseas. While I was out to dinner one evening with our host committee, my purse was stolen. As we were sitting there talking about the things of God, a thief eased in and took my valuable possessions. I couldn't believe it! I knew it was more than an isolated incident. The Lord revealed to me that I must be more vigilant because the enemy will stop at nothing to distract me, and then he'll use discouragement and disappointment to keep me wallowing in my misfortune.

Later, as I was getting into bed, the Lord impressed upon me to grab paper and pencil (which I always keep by my bedside for such moments). I was impressed to write as many negative D words as I could think of. I wrote these: *Disappointment. Discouragement. Debt. Disbelief. Divorce. Depression. Disease. Disagreement. Death. Depravity. Danger. Distraction.* (I'm sure you can think of more negative D words as you read this.) I found that there is a connection to these negative words. It is quite easy for these words and attitudes to find their way into our conversations and ways of thinking. Satan uses these negative D words as tools to keep God's people from realizing victory in our lives. But God's word shows me that He has an answer for every *D* word we may face.

For example, you may be waiting on God for a miracle, but the results seem slow in coming to pass. When this happens, you may be tempted to say, "Oh well, I *doubt* it's ever going to happen." In such times you must remember Philippians 1:6: "I am confident of this very thing, that He who began a good work in [me] will perfect it until the day of Christ Jesus" (NASB).

From time to time, you may feel the pangs of *discouragement* rising up in your heart. Squelch that negative emotion by building yourself up with the promise from Psalm 42:5-6:

> Why am I so sad?
>> Why am I so upset?
> I should put my hope in God
>> and keep praising him,
>> my Savior and my God. (NCV)

Your enemy aims to *decimate* your hopes, *deprive* you of your joy, and *destroy* your health. Remember Jesus came "that [you] might have life, and . . . have it more abundantly" (John 10:10).

When *disagreement* plagues your relationship, remember 1 Peter 4:8: "Above all, love each other deeply, because love covers over a multitude of sins" (NIV).

When you find it *difficult* to concentrate and you battle with *distraction*, stand on the promise that "thou wilt keep him in perfect peace, whose mind is stayed on thee" (Isaiah 26:3).

DON'T FALTER

For every tool Satan uses to come against you, Jesus has a powerful weapon you can use to fight back. That weapon is God's word. Don't give in or let down your guard. Instead take up your rightful position as a blood-bought, born-again, Spirit-filled child of God, and stand on the power of God's word. Your position is one of an equipped and powerful warrior. From head to toe, you are to put on the whole armor of God. "Hanging in there" is not allowed. We must not hang in there, as some are in the habit of saying casually. The phrase seems harmless, but words have power and life! So I've taken that phrase *hang in there* out of my vocabulary. I refuse to use it because hanging in there is never the stance of the believer. God's word never said, "Just hang in there and see God's salvation." God never said, "You just hang in there until I can get back with you." No!

We are commanded to "*stand* . . . and see the salvation of the LORD," according to 2 Chronicles 20:17. Ephesians 6:13 tells us again, "Having done all, to *stand*." Ephesians 6:14 reiterates it: "*Stand* therefore." (My emphasis has been added to each verse here.) You must never compromise your position. You don't have to hang in there because Jesus already did that for you when He hung on the cross at Calvary. He was hung up for your hang-ups so you could stand up confidently on His word. So speak these words to yourself right now: "No longer will I take the position of hanging in there. From now on I'm standing in there!"

Don't let the unknown details concerning tomorrow fill your heart with fear and cause you to trip and fall. God has already taken care of tomorrow. Don't let the enemy deceive you. With God on your side, how can you lose?

DON'T FLEE

The possibility is great that you face some sort of conflict today. If there is a challenge in your life, don't run from it, no matter how difficult it may be. With God's help, meet your challenges head-on. The children of Judah had every reason to run for cover. Instead they received instructions from the Lord on how to endure the battle. Read how they carried out those instructions:

> When [Jehoshaphat] had consulted with the people, he appointed singers unto the LORD, and that should praise the beauty of holiness, as they went out before the army, and to say, Praise the LORD; for his mercy endureth for ever. And when they began to sing and to praise, the Lord set ambushments against the children of Ammon, Moab, and mount Seir, which were come against Judah; and they were smitten. (2 Chronicles 20:21-22)

God's instructions may be a bit unconventional. Obey them nevertheless. The Lord told the children of Judah to praise their way out instead of fight. Why? Praise confuses the enemy. Praise is like pouring salt in Satan's wounds. As the heavenly worship leader, he was kicked out of heaven when he became proud. He will never have that privilege again. That blessed privilege has been given to you as a child of the Most High God. Shake your fist in the face of the enemy by giving God praise, even before you know the outcome. So what if you don't have a singer's voice? That's not a requirement! Open your mouth, speak the praises of God, and watch the enemy run!

You may have been praying, asking God to answer a specific request. Here is an assignment for you. As you wait on God, *wait* on God. Picture yourself with a white linen napkin draped across your arm, giving God the best of your service. Just as a well-trained waiter would attend to your every need while waiting on your table in a fine restaurant, you are to serve the Lord with joy, even anticipating His desires. Just as you reward the waiter for fine service after enjoying a great meal, God will fortify you with just what you need: "They that wait upon the

LORD shall renew their strength; they shall mount up with wings as eagles; they shall run and not be weary; and they shall walk, and not faint" (Isaiah 40:31).

This passage of scripture is a favorite among Christians. We love to highlight it in our Bibles. We say "amen" when we hear it quoted. And sometimes, we believe that the wonderful blessings we read about in this passage come to us simply as a result of God's goodness to us. We love the idea of having renewed strength, soaring with eagles, running and never getting tired, and walking without growing weak. But what does this mean? Certainly we do get weak. Sometimes we behave more like chickens than eagles. (And sometimes like chickens with their heads cut off!) We do get tired from the dailiness of life and weary from our challenges. This scripture teaches us that the benefits come, not just because God is good but because we *wait* on God, who is good. Could it be that you are not soaring high with the eagles or running the race without getting weary or going the distance without becoming faint because you have not learned the value of the race?

If you are waiting on God to follow through on His promise to you, don't worry or become impatient and resort to your own plan. Don't lag behind. Don't get anxious and get ahead of God. This one thing is for certain: you cannot hurry God. He follows His own clock. And He will always come through right on time.

Do you believe God loves you? Do you believe He cares deeply for you? He does, you know. Then place all your trust in Him and wait patiently for Him. This I know for sure: you are not to fear but to look for the promises He has in store for you. As you read this promise from the Lord, insert your name among God's people, who are addressed directly here in Isaiah 43:1:

> Now, says the LORD—
>   the one who created [your name],
>   the one who formed [your name]:
> Don't fear, for I have redeemed you;
>   I have called you by name; you are mine. (CEB)

CHAPTER 9

IN THE LEAN TIMES

God, listen to my cry;
pay attention to my prayer!
When my heart is weak,
I cry out to you
from the very ends of the earth.
Lead me to the rock
that is higher than I am
because you have been my refuge.
—Psalm 61:1-3 CEB

Nestled within the pages of the Gospel of Luke is an account so brief, if you weren't looking for it, you might easily overlook it. It is the story of a woman from the town of Nain. This woman had lost everything she considered valuable. The husband she loved for years had died, leaving her a widow, and death came knocking at her door again to claim the life of her only son, way too early in his young adult life. She was on her way to bury the young man, who had been her sole means of support since the death of her husband, and who had no doubt been the bright spot in a dark season of her life. Without a male family member to meet her needs, the days ahead would certainly be difficult for her. Like most widows, she would face extreme poverty.

The times had not been kind to this woman. She was left alone and lonely in her grief. She had been robbed of her joy, stripped of her dignity, cheated of her dreams, and drained of her hopes, her heart and her arms empty. This nameless widow knew what it was like to be down—down in the dumps, down to her last dime, and down on her luck. *But.* (Don't you just love the word *but*? In the same way we discovered that there is always a promise behind the words *fear not*, you can always anticipate that something really exciting is waiting on the other side of the word *but*.) But—this is what I know for sure— God does His best work when we are down.

Yes, when we are down to nothing, God is up to something.

JESUS WILL COME TO YOU

The Bible mentions many widows throughout the Old and New Testaments, paying special recognition to them and admonishing us to honor and care for them. This widow's story is found in Luke 7:11-16. (Luke was the only writer of the Gospels to record this account.) Shortly before encountering the widow and her deceased son, Jesus entered Capernaum. It was there that Jesus healed a centurion's servant after the centurion had heard that Jesus was nearby. The Lord had only to send His word with messengers, and the miracle occurred. Imagine that. Jesus, the living Word, sent the spoken word, with power, and it was accomplished. Then we find the story of the widow whom Jesus helped in her lowest hour:

> Now it happened, the day after, that He went into a city called Nain; and many of His disciples went with Him, and a larger crowd. And when He came near the gate of the city, behold, a dead man was being carried out, the only son of his mother; and she was a widow. And a large crowd from the city was with her. When the Lord saw her, He had compassion on her and said to her, "Do not weep." Then He came and touched the open coffin, and those who carried him stood still. And He said, "Young man, I say to you, arise." So he who was dead sat up and began to speak. And He presented him to his mother. Then fear came upon all, and they glorified God, saying "A great prophet has risen up among us"; and "God has visited His people." (NKJV™)

Oh, don't you wish you could have been there to witness Jesus raising this young man from the dead? I would have loved to have been a part of the masses that followed Jesus on His preaching and teaching tour around the Sea of Galilee. Today, all over Hollywood, people and paparazzi are hoping to catch a glimpse of their favorite actors and rock stars as they are out and about on the city street. Wherever Jesus was, He drew a crowd. A growing number of disciples, the sick and infirm, curiosity seekers, and religious skeptics followed Him. Jesus had been going about, healing the sick, casting out demons, and teaching the multitudes, but this day would stand out among the rest. This would be the first display of His power to bring the dead to life again. The miracles of raising Jairus's daughter and Lazarus would follow later. Other prophets like Elijah and Elisha had raised the dead, but it was God who used them in these circumstances. So when the people witnessed Jesus' powerful act, they knew that He was no ordinary man, but a man sent from God.

This is what I love about Jesus. This woman, so distraught by her loss, so engulfed in her sorrow, so engrossed in her pain, did not even see Jesus as He approached. Oh, but you can be certain He saw her. She did not come to where He was, seeking Him out. He came to where she was. Isn't that just like Jesus? He came down to our level because we could not get up to His. He put on flesh and became like us so we could put on a robe of righteousness and become like Him. From the moment He saw her in the funeral procession, head hung low, dressed in funeral garb, back bent with grief so heavy it could actually be felt, He had compassion for her. Jesus always has compassion for those who are grieving from a loss.

After a recent concert, I met a precious young lady who stood waiting in line to speak to me. While others waited to get their CDs and books signed or to get a picture taken, she had nothing in her hand. What she did have was a story in her heart. She had recently had a miscarriage and could hardly get the painful words out before she began to cry. I wasted no time, embracing her tightly, comforting her, calling on Jesus to heal her pain. What a privilege it was to bear her burden if only for a few moments.

Dear friend, are you burdened today? If that is the case, you can have complete confidence in knowing that whenever you are at a loss, Jesus feels your pain, and He has compassion for you. As frail human beings, we can only assist in burden bearing for each other for a little while before we are distracted by our own discomforts. But Jesus will carry not only the burden; He will carry you *and* your burden as long and as far as you need and not one moment or one step short of going the full distance. Not only that, when you have exhausted all your resources and you don't have the strength to go another single, solitary step, take comfort in this: just as Jesus did for this widow, He will meet you right where you are. And just like a mother who drops whatever it is she is doing to comfort her hurting child, He will speak the same beautiful words He spoke to the widow: "Don't cry."

JESUS WILL CARE FOR YOU

In the hand-hewn open coffin lay the body of the widow's son, wrapped in a sheet. Jesus did what was unheard of, particularly for a rabbi. He touched the dead body. Most rabbis wouldn't think of touching the dead for fear of being considered unclean. But with Jesus, the Teacher of teachers, the Resurrection and the Life, even the dead obey His voice. And the living? They, too, are halted by His authority. The pallbearers and those in the funeral procession stopped to experience the demonstration of His power.

Jesus spoke to the dead man and told him to "arise" (v. 14). And at His word, the young man sat up and began to speak. Can you imagine how amazed His followers must have been? And the widow! Imagine the depth of her joy at the return of her son. This mother had no idea what would happen and who she would meet as she left her home for the grave site that day. One thing I love about Jesus is that He is full of wonderful surprises. When you least expect it, He manifests His presence, bringing light to darkness, life to death, and joy to sorrow.

I've sung for a lot of funerals in my lifetime. Singing under these circumstances is never easy. Choosing just the right song is always a challenge. But if I were in the crowd that day and had been asked to sing at that funeral, I would have had to change my tune. Out with "Nearer My God to Thee"! After seeing that young man come back from the dead, I would have led a rousing rendition of the "Hallelujah Chorus." You see, Jesus never attended a funeral where the dead stayed dead. He has all power, even power over death, so when Jesus comes to a funeral, the funeral is over. Once the dead are raised to life again, there's nothing left to do but celebrate. Jesus blesses exceedingly, abundantly, above all we could ask or think (Ephesians 3:20).

JESUS WILL CARRY YOU

Jesus spoke to the deceased young man, and that young man sat up and began to talk (Luke 7:15). Wouldn't you like to know what that young man's first words were? Maybe he exclaimed something like, "Boy, that was the best nap ever. I slept like a rock!" Or maybe his words were a series of questions such as, "Who are all these people? Why am I in a casket? What did You say Your name was, Sir?"

Whatever his words, it's easy to imagine that both the mother and the son gave endless thanks and praise to Jesus for what He had done. These events caused them, and those around them, to want to know more about Jesus and the life-changing truths He taught. The crowd of followers was astounded at this, His first resurrection miracle. The story concludes by saying that fear had come upon all the people, and they glorified God, for in Christ they saw the hope they had long been awaiting. They saw the power of possibility that could carry them from where they were to places they had only dreamed of before.

What's your story? Is there anything that has died in your life? Do you have a dead, passionless marriage that makes you feel more like a roommate than a wife? Maybe you've been told your womb is lifeless, causing you to die just a little more each day on the inside. Are you working a dead-end job with no hope for promotion? Do you have a mountain of debt and not a bit of credit? Relax. You see, Jesus is best known for breathing life back into situations that have been pronounced dead on arrival. He can resurrect dead hopes and transform dashed dreams. He is able to reignite the fires of faith if you are hesitant to believe. And He can restore your joy if you feel that you are in the pit of despair.

What has been lost in your life today? If you need renewing, relieving, restoring, reviving, or resurrecting and you have no other recourse, no other resources, come to Jesus, and trust in Him for comfort and refuge. The psalmist David is a beloved songwriter and author whose works and words consistently bring me comfort and encouragement. He expresses the depth of emotion we all have felt during our lowest moments. Listen to his words from Psalm 61:

> Hear my cry, O God;
>> listen to my prayer.
> From the ends of the earth I call to you,
>> I call as my heart grows faint;
>> lead me to the rock that is higher than I.
> For you have been my refuge,
>> a strong tower against the foe. (vv. 1-3 NIV)

In the song that inspired this book, "This I Know for Sure," my desire is to voice the inner longings of the soul. The lyrics of the third verse of the song and the chorus that follows come to my mind at this time. Let them encourage your heart:

> When the nights are lonesome
> Fear comes with dismay
> I find peace in His presence
> And strength again to say
>
> There is a God in Heaven
> And I am in His plan
> He will forsake me never
> My life is in His hands
> His boundless love will lead me
> As long as time endures
> Oh, this I know
> This I know for sure

GOD WILL ALWAYS FIND A WAY

What do you know for sure, dear friend? You can add this to the list: God's people can always find comfort and encouragement in Him when times are hardest. For some, the times have never been leaner. For many of you, times are tight, the cupboards are bare, the gas tank is empty, and the kids need new shoes. For others, you may be one or two paychecks from hard times. No matter what the situation, God will always find a way.

When love has died, the house is quiet, the nights are long, and hope seems all but gone, lean in and listen closely for a still, small voice. Jesus has something He wants you to know for sure. He wants you to know that you are not forsaken. When Jesus is all you have, He is all you need. Do you believe this?

He is the comforter for those who mourn. He is the healer for those who are sick. He is a shelter in the storm. He is the Way when there seems to be no way. So when you feel you have nothing left, don't despair. Remember what Jesus did for the widow and her son. Then remember this: when you are down to nothing, God is up to something.

PART FOUR

THERE IS A GOD IN HEAVEN
AND I AM IN HIS PLAN
HE WILL FORSAKE ME NEVER

My life is in His hands

His boundless love will lead me
As long as time endures
Oh, this I know
This I know for sure

Lord, my times are in thy hand;
All my fondest hopes have planned,
To thy wisdom I resign,
And would make thy purpose mine.

Thou my daily task shall give;
Day by day to thee I live:
So shall added years fulfill,
Not my own, my Father's will.

Fond ambition, whisper not;
Happy is my humble lot;
Anxious, busy cares, away;
I'm provided for to-day.

Oh, to live exempt from care,
By the energy of prayer,
Strong in faith, with mind subdued,
Yet elate with gratitude.

—Josiah Conder[1]

CHAPTER 10

THE PASSION OF FAITH

Lord, listen carefully to the prayer of your servant and the prayers of your
servants who love to honor you. Give me, your servant, success today;
allow this king to show kindness to me.

—Nehemiah 1:11 NCV

Early in my ministry, I was invited to sing at one of the women's jails in the Atlanta area. There was no meeting room at the facility, so my hosts and I improvised by setting up a stage area at the front of a small jail cell, large enough to hold only three wooden bleachers bolted to the floor. There, among the iron bars, I set up a portable sound system and prepared music and an encouraging message from God's word to share with the inmates. Since it was not possible to sing for a larger group of women all at once, the officers of the jail permitted smaller groups of women to come into the holding cell for fifteen to twenty minutes at a time for a series of miniconcerts.

In groups of five or six, women of every age and race, shackled and chained together at the hands and feet, were led into that cell where I could minister the hope and the love of Jesus to them for a few moments. I sang for about six groups of women, and each time I sang and spoke before these women—somebody's mother, daughter, sister, grandmother, granddaughter, or friend—I didn't hold anything back. I sang as if I were on stage at Madison Square Garden. I thought that prison bars might open up and set prisoners free, just as they did when Paul and Silas sang praises to God at midnight (Acts 16). The praises were glorious.

During each miniconcert the women and I sang and worshiped together. We laughed and cried together, and each time I had the privilege of praying for the women, leading some to accept the Lord Jesus as Savior. By the time I had delivered the last miniconcert, I had sung for about thirty-five women. My prayer that day was that the hearts of the women who came to that sanctuary in a jail cell would be touched and changed. I know of one woman specifically whose heart was forever changed—me! That was a very precious time of ministry for me, and I left the jail with a real sense of purpose, determined to do my part in leading women everywhere to Jesus. Some might consider those women hopeless cases, but I gave them every reason to believe that with Jesus, there is no hopeless case. They, in turn, gave me thirty-five reasons to be passionate about women's ministry.

You see, when you seek to add significance to someone else's life, it adds significance to *your* life. If ever there was a man who was determined to make his life count, that man was Nehemiah, whose story appears in the Old Testament. A highly respected leader, the royal cupbearer to King Artaxerxes of Persia, Nehemiah was noted to be a dedicated and trustworthy man who gained tremendous favor and the friendship of the king. If you want to know what it looks like when a man places everything in God's hands, Nehemiah is the one to examine. He had firm resolve, with strong hands and a tender heart; he was devoted to God and the people he loved, and we have much to learn from his life.

NEHEMIAH HAD PASSION

Although he enjoyed a comfortable lifestyle under the king's authority in Persia, Nehemiah was still a Hebrew servant, a slave in the king's palace. He lived far away from Jerusalem, but his heart longed for the land of his heritage, his hopes, and his dreams. While many Jews who lived in Persia during the Babylonian captivity assimilated and became like the culture around them, Nehemiah chose to serve God rather than men. Nehemiah shows us how, when we live a life that pleases God, it may not be comfortable, popular, or convenient. He cared about none of those things. He cared only about doing what was right: remaining faithful to God and the mission assigned to him from on high.

When Nehemiah received word that far-off Jerusalem's walls were in dilapidated condition and its city gates burned, his heart was broken. In those days, a city with a well-built wall system was fortified; on the other hand, a city without walls was at dire risk and exposed to its enemies (kind of like leaving the windows and doors of your house wide open when you leave for work). Nehemiah wrote,

> One of my brothers named Hanani came with some other men from Judah. I asked them about Jerusalem and the Jewish people who lived through the captivity. They answered me, "Those who are left from the captivity are back in Judah, but they are in much trouble and are full of shame. The wall around Jerusalem is broken down, and its gates have been burned." When I heard these things, I sat down and cried for several days. I was sad and fasted. I prayed to the God of heaven, "LORD, God of heaven, you are the great God who is to be respected. You are loyal, and you keep your agreement with those who love you and obey your commands. (Nehemiah 1:2-5 NCV)

When we read the book of Nehemiah, it's as if we are peering over his shoulder to read an entry from his personal journal. Do you recognize the pattern of prayer here that is so customary of the godly people we read about in God's word? Nehemiah began his prayer by worshiping God, just as Daniel, Jehoshaphat, and so many others did. He continued: "LORD, listen carefully to the prayer of your servant and the prayers of your servants who love to honor you. Give me, your servant, success today; allow this king to show kindness to me" (1:11 NCV).

Nehemiah was so deeply grieved by the condition of his people that he took his burden immediately to God in prayer. He loved his homeland, but what could he do from so far away? His heart was broken, but he was moved to do something. Have you ever been so burdened by a people, a church, a family, a school, or a city that it broke your heart and drew you to tears? That burden you feel is the Lord moving upon your heart to become involved and to be a conduit, a catalyst, for change.

Take your cue from Nehemiah and see how your misery may open the door to your ministry. What is your response to the things that burden your heart? Do you respond in anger or frustration? Do you throw up your hands and walk away? Do you worry and complain that somebody ought to do something about the problem? Or do you immediately go to God in prayer to ask how you can do your part?

For some of us, *ministry* may sound like a big, scary word, but it means "to help." An old adage says, "Preach the gospel at all times. Use words, when necessary." Friend, Jesus isn't looking for more church folk to warm a pew. He's looking for ambassadors to spread His love throughout the earth. If God is prompting you to do something, don't delay another moment, dear friend. Initiate a conversation with God about His assignment for you. Follow Nehemiah's lead. By faith he took his burden to God. By faith he received a plan from the Lord. And by faith he would carry out the plan.

NEHEMIAH HAD A MISSION

Nehemiah gave God an open invitation to use him to save his people and rebuild Jerusalem. The Lord heard Nehemiah's prayer and moved upon the heart of King Artaxerxes, who not only gave his blessing for Nehemiah to go but also donated all the supplies to be used in the building project. Then he provided the proper letters of authority to permit Nehemiah to pass through other lands on his way to Judah. The king sent army officers and soldiers along with him to validate the king's authority and ensure safe passage.

Once he arrived in Jerusalem, Nehemiah wasted no time. He immediately began assessing the excessive damages that had been done to his beloved city. With care and concern, he devised a plan and shared it with the people: "I said to them, 'You can see the trouble we have here. Jerusalem is a pile of ruins, and its gates have been burned. Come, let's rebuild the wall of Jerusalem so we won't be full of shame any longer.' I also told them how God had been kind to me and what the king had said to me. Then they answered, 'Let's start rebuilding' " (Nehemiah 2:17-18 NCV).

And so the work began.

Have you ever been faced with a huge challenge? Your answer is probably yes. Going into that challenge, did you know how things were going to work out? Your answer is probably no. There is no way to know the outcome to every problem. That is where your faith in Jesus Christ comes in. Hebrews 11:1 is a landmark passage that can give you strength and encouragement: "Now faith is the substance of things hoped for, the evidence of things not seen." I also appreciate the way the New Century Version defines *faith*: "Faith means being sure of the things we hope for and knowing that something is real even if we do not see it."

Faith is much more than just believing in God. Faith believes God will do just as He promised, even though you might not see any evidence. Faith isn't passive. *Faith* is a verb; it's an action word. It's a demonstration of your trust in the Lord. So it requires a response on your part. I grew up hearing the saints in my father's church say, "If you make one step, He'll make two." Sure, there are times when you are too weak to fight and you couldn't take another step if your life depended on it. God knows that, and He is there for you in those times. But there comes a time when you must do as Nehemiah did. You must get up, get dressed, get a plan, and get to work. You must take off your Sunday best and put on your coveralls and work boots because James 2:20 tells us that "faith without works is dead."

Do you know someone in need? Is there a mission or a ministry that needs your support? Could a friend or neighbor use a personal visit or a phone call of encouragement? You can do the work of Jesus as you put your faith into action. When you do this, an amazing thing will happen. You will find that faith is not just believing that the power of God can change the world, but faith is believing that the power of God can change the world through *you*!

NEHEMIAH FACED OPPOSITION

Whenever you step out in faith, you'll encounter a foe. There will always be opposition whenever it's time to do anything for the kingdom of God. Nehemiah encountered his share of foes for sure: "When Sanballat heard we were rebuilding the wall, he was very angry, even furious. He made fun of the Jewish people" (Nehemiah 4:1 NCV). Nehemiah's enemies, even people with power and influence, banded together to try to stop his progress. His challengers resorted to mockery, mudslinging, and name-calling:

> He said to his friends and those with power in Samaria, "What are these weak Jews doing? Will they rebuild the wall? Will they offer sacrifices? Can they finish it in one day? Can they bring stones back to life from piles of trash and ashes?" Tobiah the Ammonite, who was next to Sanballat, said, "If a fox climbed up on the stone wall they are building, it would break it down." (Nehemiah 4:2-3 NCV)

I've found this to be true: whenever I've attempted to do anything at all for Jesus, I've encountered some sort of difficulty. I've been in ministry for thirty years as a full-time vocation, longer than that if you count the years that I was bivocational, singing while teaching school. At every turn I encountered some sort of opposition from the adversary. I've experienced challenges in my marriage. At times, it was difficult maintaining a family and a growing ministry. My husband has had challenges with his health. There have been times I've been very discouraged. So, difficulties are a given. As a matter of fact, I've come to expect difficulty. I take it as a compliment that I must be doing something right.

I'm not alone in this. The Apostle Paul said, "I find it to be a law that when I want to do right, evil lies close at hand" (Romans 7:21 ESV). You see, Satan, the enemy of your faith, is a great deceiver; he is relentlessly looking for a way to cheat you out of your blessings. But Jesus is the Great Deliverer. Whenever you bring your faith in Jesus and the truth of His word into your circumstances, Satan's plot is exposed, and his plan is destroyed.

Satan's kingdom represents darkness while God's kingdom represents light. So the very moment darkness poses a threat to you, bring the light of Jesus into the situation and darkness will have to flee (James 4:7). It's just like walking into a darkened room and flipping on the light switch. The second you do that, the darkness is overcome. It's gone! When light fills the room, anything that lives in the dark runs for cover. The devil may try to intimidate you by causing you to be fearful. Don't be afraid. Move closer to Jesus and the light of His promises. If you are discouraged, bring the presence of Jesus into your situation by encouraging yourself in the Lord (as David did in 1 Samuel 30:6).

Whenever you are tempted to doubt what God has said, use the authority that Jesus gave you by opening your mouth to speak the truth of His word. You see, the devil has no power unless you cooperate with him. If you don't give him any ground, Satan is dead in the water. With Jesus on your side, the devil is already a defeated foe. This is why it is so important that you know the word of God. Jesus said, "You will know the truth, and the truth will set you free" (John 8:32 NIV). Owning a Bible won't set you free. But *knowing* the truth and standing on what you know will *empower* you, not only to wage war against the enemy's assaults but also to win!

Nehemiah and God's people could've thrown in the towel and quit building. Mocked, cheated, laughed at, mistreated—it didn't matter. The naysayers' threats didn't deter the people of God from their mission. The opposition only empowered them and gave them more determination to complete the work:

> Sanballat, Tobiah, Geshem the Arab, and our other enemies heard that I had rebuilt the wall and that there was not one gap in it. But I had not yet set the doors in the gates. So Sanballat and Geshem sent me this message: "Come, Nehemiah, let's meet together in Kephirim on the plain of Ono." But they were planning to harm me. So I sent messengers to them with this answer: "I am doing a great work, and I can't come down." (Nehemiah 6:1-3 NCV)

Do you hear Nehemiah's dogged determination and tenacity? He was not about to allow anything to keep him from rebuilding that wall, and their mission was completed in fifty-two days! Oh, dear friend, what is the wall that God has assigned you to build today? Are there influences in our culture that are trying to dissuade you from building your marriage and family? Your response has to be, "I am doing a great work, and I can't come down." Are you trying to get a business off the ground? No matter what you come up against, you must endeavor to say, "I am doing a great work, and I can't come down." Are you working on your finances, trying to lose weight, getting free from an addiction? Don't let anything stop you. Speak to anything and everything that is standing in your way: "I am doing a great work, and I can't come down."

There's something powerful about setting God's word to music. When scripture is set to music, the message not only adheres to your memory; it gets in your spirit too. Then as you hear yourself singing it, it brings strength to your soul. That's why I love to set the word of God to music. I was inspired to write a song about Nehemiah, so I got together with my dear friend and songwriting buddy Turner Lawton. She and I wrote a song about this great man of God who rebuilt the wall around the city of Jerusalem. It's called "Stay Up on the Wall." Let me share the chorus with you:

Stay up on the wall
And don't come down
You've got too much work to do
No time to turn around
With a hammer in one hand
And a weapon in the other
My sister, my brother
Stay up on the wall[1]

NEHEMIAH PRAYED

Have you ever looked back over the course of your life and wondered how you arrived at the place where you are now? All we have to do is look at Nehemiah's life, and we can see how one thought set the course for his whole life. The philosopher and psychologist William James said it best: "To sow a thought is to reap an action, to sow an action is to reap a habit, to sow a habit is to reap a character, and to sow a character is to reap a destiny."[2]

So, does your thought life need an overhaul? Do you want to establish new habits or set new goals? Nehemiah shows us that talking to God is the first step in making your life count, so I challenge you to join me in praying this prayer:

God, show me where my place is on the wall. How can I participate in rebuilding the walls of strength and protection in my life? What is the mission that you desire for me to complete? Have I been complacent or neglectful or avoided areas that really need attention now? God, will You give me a passion, a deep desire, to help others? To help myself? Then, Lord, I give You permission to take that passion and turn it into a burden. Lord, maybe I could help single moms, older citizens, or those who are incarcerated. Maybe I could mentor kids on the street or spend more time with my family. Maybe I need to fortify the walls of my marriage, get out of debt, or complete my education. Help me, Lord, to get toxic people out of my life. Whatever it is, Lord, open my eyes to see the places in my life that have been torn down and left in ruins. Help me to see the relationships that need repair or the situations concerning my health that need to change. Help me to develop the mind-set that passion and problems go hand in hand. So, here I am, Lord, turning my life over to You. I allow You to place a hammer in one hand and the weapon of Your word in the other. Thank You for helping me to find my place in Your great work. In Jesus' name, amen.

By observing Nehemiah's life, we learn how to rebuild and restore the things that are broken down in our lives. The qualities that Nehemiah possessed, although he was not a typical man, are not reserved only for a special brand or breed of people. The same qualities are meant for you! You see, there is a special mission assigned to you. There is a specific work God desires you to build up.

Should you choose to accept that mission, at first you may feel intimidated. But remember, you don't have to help *everybody*. Just help *somebody*. You don't have to do *everything*. Just do *one thing*. Help the widow next door; encourage the pregnant teenager; coach the kid who has no dad at home; teach the Sunday school class. You'll find that once you give God something to work with, God will bless and multiply your talents. In His divine presence, He will empower you to carry out that mission until it's completed.

Have you found your passion in life? Is that passion a driving force that motivates you to help others? This I know for sure: as you build up people, you are being built up. When you come to God with ready hands and a willing heart, who knows where He might lead? Happy building, dear friend!

CHAPTER 11

THE PROMISE OF FAITH

*[The LORD] brought Abram outside and said, "Look up at the sky and
count the stars if you think you can count them." He continued, "This
is how many children you will have." Abram trusted the LORD, and the
LORD recognized Abram's high moral character."*
—Genesis 15:5-6 CEB

One of the greatest men I ever knew was my grandfather
Pastor John Wade. Born in the Deep South at the close
of the nineteenth century, he grew up the son of a preacher and
served God from his youth. He was one of nine children, and
his family progressed as farmers, educators, and entrepreneurs.

They married, raised families, and thrived despite tremendous racial indifference and the economic hardship they endured as black people in Alabama. No stranger to hard work, my grandfather was extremely ambitious, exercising tremendous resilience during those early days of the second Industrial Revolution. But tough times didn't make him a bitter man; tough times made him a better man. He possessed a deep, vibrant faith in Christ, along with strength of character and a resolve of steel.

Once God called him to preach, he became a powerful minister of the gospel with a voracious hunger for the things of God. His recall of the Scriptures was remarkable; he was able to recite entire passages from the Bible. His understanding of the Scriptures, his ability to interpret the truths of the word of God, and his fiery preaching were things to behold. My grandfather visited us from time to time at our home in Jackson, Michigan, and people came from far and wide to hear him preach as he led revivals at my father's church. Papa Wade, as we called him, was a Baptist pastor for many years in Mississippi, where he lived with my grandmother until she passed away. After that, he lived as a single man until a dear lady caught his eye. He took her as his bride when he was close to eighty years of age.

My grandfather continued to preach and pastor well into his eighties, pastoring four congregations in neighboring towns, which he visited on the same Sunday once a month. One fifth Sunday morning, he was the guest preacher at a nearby church (he had accepted the invitation since he had no appointment that Sunday), and when it was time to deliver the sermon, he stirred every heart as he preached with power and conviction about faith in Christ. After delivering that soul-stirring sermon,

Papa Wade sat down in the pulpit, drew his last breath, and went home to be with the Lord. He was a remarkable man, who preached his own eulogy while he lived. I will always remember him and his deep love for Christ, his family, and the church. He lived as a man of faith and died in the same manner.

That is my heart's desire—to be a person of great faith and conviction who will not be swayed, no matter what comes my way! In the introduction, I told you my purpose for writing this book: that you would know God intimately through a personal relationship with Jesus Christ and take Him at His word without wavering. Is that your desire? You see, faith is a most vital ingredient to your Christian growth. Remember Hebrews 11:1? "Now faith is the substance of things hoped for, the evidence of things not seen." Not only must you have faith, but faith must have you! In this crazy, mixed-up world we're living in, only your faith and belief in Christ Jesus will keep you grounded. It's like a fishing boat on the open waters. It can withstand the storm and rains. Why? Because it has an anchor that will hold it steady.

Your greatest responsibility and calling are to believe God. Jesus said, "This is the work of God, that ye believe on him whom he hath sent" (John 6:29). Believing on Jesus is the only way to realize eternal life: "These are written, that ye might believe that Jesus is the Christ, the Son of God; and that believing ye might have life through his name" (John 20:31). The eloquent preacher Charles Haddon Spurgeon said, "Little faith will bring your souls to heaven, but great faith will bring heaven to your souls."[1] That is my deepest desire! My prayer is to possess greater faith, which opens the door and makes room for more of God in my life.

GOD'S APPEAL

Abraham stands out in the Bible as one of the greatest men the world has ever known. He is known for his deep and abiding faith in God. So much so that he is called "the father of all them that believe" (Romans 4:11) and "the Friend of God" (James 2:23). His name is loved and highly esteemed by Christians and Jews alike.

We read about Abraham's great faith in Hebrews 11, otherwise known as the Hall of Faith. The pastor and author Adrian Rogers said, "When you came to Jesus Christ, God enrolled you in the school of faith. Life is the classroom, the Bible is the textbook, the apostles and the prophets are the professors, and Abraham would have to be the dean in this school of faith."[2] If you are a Christian, you are considered a student of faith. So pull up your assigned seat, lean in, and listen. I believe God wants to speak to your heart. If you desire to live a life of faith, taking God as at His word without wavering, you must believe God's word.

Are you aware that you can know for sure how to live a life that is well pleasing to God? Following Abraham's example will help you not only to better understand God's purpose for your life but also to fulfill that plan. Let's read what Hebrews 11:8 tells us about Abraham: "By faith Abraham, when he was called to go out into a place which he should after receive for an inheritance, obeyed; and he went out, not knowing whither he went."

Abraham was not a perfect man, but he shows us that a life of faith is not only noble; it is necessary. Verse 8 tells us that Abraham was *attentive to God's voice*. An important dynamic occurs here. God called, and Abraham answered the call. This means that Abraham was in a position to hear God's voice. What an outstanding lesson for us in this noisy, postmillennial age of reality television, Internet streaming, infomercials, and twenty-four-hour news channels. Just look around you at this moment. How many potential distractions are within arm's reach? A ringing cell phone? A blaring television? An electronic listening device of some kind? A wandering thought? How many times have you heard the annoying ringtone of a cell phone right in the middle of a Sunday morning worship service? It always seems to ring at the precise moment the congregation has paused to pray.

Not long ago Charles and I were out to dinner. Sitting at a nearby table was a family of four. Instead of enjoying the company of family, engaging in conversation concerning the day's activities, each of them totally ignored the others, their food growing cold, while they buried their faces in their cell phones. Is it any wonder we cannot hear God's voice? We are too preoccupied with so many things. I'm not saying to do away with cell phones, TV, music, and the like. Not at all. It's OK to enjoy these things. Just be careful that you are not consumed by them. There's no harm in owning this stuff. But be careful that your stuff doesn't own you.

Dear friend, God desires to speak to you concerning His will and His ways. He is speaking to you at this very moment. If you want to hear what God is saying to your heart, turn off the noise. Rid yourself of distractions. Remember Psalm 46:10: "Be still, and know that I am God." He is always speaking, but His voice doesn't always sound like rolling thunder or crashing seas. Sometimes he speaks in the colorful hues of the evening sunset. At times He whispers in the soothing showers of a spring rain. You may hear his voice in the refrain of an old hymn. Whenever you sense His gentle nudge, stop and enjoy His presence.

ABRAHAM'S ANSWER

At nearly every turn, Abraham demonstrated a life of faithfulness. *He submitted to God's vision* although he didn't understand all the details of God's instructions. In the Bible, God often required that people separate themselves from the country and the people they loved. God required this of Abraham. Read Hebrews 11:8 once more: "By faith Abraham, when he was called to go out into a place which he should after receive for an inheritance, obeyed; and he went out, not knowing whither he went."

Abraham left the country he loved and the people he deeply cared about to venture into the unknown—to a place he had never seen before—and he would never return to his homeland. Can you imagine your spouse rushing home today to tell you to start packing? You don't know exactly why you're going, but you'll immediately be moving to an unknown destination and you won't be coming back. Basically, that's what happened with Abraham. He and Sarah packed up and moved with no idea of where they were headed. They didn't know how long they would be gone. They had no idea who they would meet along the way. There was no way to know what was waiting for them around the next bend. God called, and without question, Abraham obeyed. Talk about faith!

The story goes that one day a mother called her child to come in from the yard and prepare for dinner. The child failed to obey his mother's voice, so she called a second time. Again the child continued to play, disobeying his mother's instruction. A third time, his mother called, but that time, she raised her voice, counted to three, called the child by his first, middle, and last names, and threatened to do bodily harm if the child didn't appear with haste. If you're a parent, you probably have a picture of what that looks like. Is that the way it is with you and your relationship with God, dear one? Are you slow to answer when the Lord speaks? Must He poke you, prod you, and even punish you before you obey His directives?

We have many opportunities to hear the voice of God today. We don't need a supernatural revelation from God to knock us off a horse, like that of Saul on the road to Damascus. We don't need to read the handwriting on the wall. We don't need to hear an audible voice like Samuel did when he was a young boy. Instead, God has given us His written word (2 Timothy 3:16). All we have to do is pick it up and read it.

We have "the mind of Christ" (1 Corinthians 2:16)! We can put what we already know into practice. And we have the help and guidance of the Holy Spirit, who will give us the wisdom we need (Isaiah 33:6). Dear friend, when God speaks, it may not make sense to you. You may not understand all the details. But know that when He speaks, don't hesitate to step out in obedience. Delayed obedience is still disobedience. Follow Abraham's example and obey. The voice of God spoke to Abraham, and the voice of God will speak to you too. Answer the Lord the moment He calls you.

THE ADVENTURE

When Abraham and Sarah ventured into the land of the unknown, they left family members, his work, and even their friends behind. Striking out into the land of promise must have seemed like a rather huge and frightening move:

> By faith [Abraham] sojourned in the land of promise, as in a strange country, dwelling in tabernacles with Isaac and Jacob, the heirs with him of the same promise; for he looked for a city which hath foundations, whose builder and maker is God. Through faith also Sarah received strength to conceive seed, and was delivered of a child when she was past age, because she judged him faithful who had promised. Therefore sprang there even of one, and him as good as dead, so many as the stars of the sky in multitude, and as the sand, which is by the sea shore innumerable. (Hebrews 11:9-13)

Through it all, Abraham continued to trust God. He knew that wherever he went, the presence of God would go with him. Abraham was committed to a faith-filled adventure with God. He would rather venture into an unfamiliar land with God than stay in a familiar place without God. You see, no matter how daunting the task God gives you, He will help you do it. You may be faced with mundane tasks that seem daunting, like paying your monthly bills or taking care of a toddler. God sees your efforts, and He will reward you for your obedience and persistence. (I have often found that as I pray and ask God to help me complete those chores that I don't look forward to, like cleaning out a closet or mopping the kitchen floor, or doing things that I find challenging, like preparing taxes, He is more than willing to help me. Most of the time, the task doesn't change or get any easier, but my attitude toward completing the task changes as I offer the work as an act of obedience to the Lord. Some of the sweetest ventures I've had with Jesus have been while I was doing housework.)

According to the Bible, Abraham was seventy-five years of age when God called him. We know that with God, age, race, marital status, and income bracket don't matter. Don't let anyone tell you that you're too old or too young. Don't allow anyone to declare that you're the wrong color or the wrong size or that you're unqualified. Don't let anybody put limits on you. Continue to obey God. He promises to bless anyone who will obey Him. In spite of the fact that Abraham and Sarah were older people, the Lord blessed Abraham and made a covenant with him: "He brought him forth abroad, and said, Look now toward heaven and tell the stars, if thou be able to number them: and he said unto him, So shall thy seed be. And he believed in the LORD; and he counted it to him for righteousness" (Genesis 15:5-6).

God promised that Abraham and Sarah would one day have a child, even though they were well past childbearing years. When Abraham was one hundred years old and Sarah was ninety, Isaac, the son promised by God, was born (Genesis 21:1-5). Look at God! He allowed a one-hundred-year-old man to father a child and a ninety-year-old woman to have a baby. Sometimes the miraculous may appear to be just plain ridiculous.

When God is at work, it may not make sense to your natural way of thinking, but this is when He is at His best. He is at His best when He is parting seas and slaying giants. He is at His best when He is bringing the dead back to life again. And He is at His best when He adds His super to your natural to do the supernatural. You see, that's how God works. He wants to make the impossible possible in your life. You just keep on believing.

Challenge your faith by praying big prayers and dreaming beyond what you can see with the natural eye. God showed Abraham the night sky and promised that his children would outnumber the stars in the heavens. In the same way, God's promises to you are far greater than you could ever comprehend. Your circumstances may change, but God is faithful and He will keep His word. He never changes. In my song "This I Know for Sure," the bridge says,

Eyes grow dim then knees get weak
How quickly seasons change
But this one thing is constant
God's love remains the same

Years may go by, situations may change, feelings may change, people may change, the odds may seem stacked against you, but when God makes a promise, He doesn't forget. And you and I are heirs of that same promise. As Abraham did, believe God for the impossible, and trust God for the invisible. Then in God's own time, He will do the incredible. Are you standing on a promise from the Lord that is yet to be realized? Are you waiting for a spouse or a child to be saved? Do you believe God can heal your body of sickness or disease? Do you trust God to carry you through a difficult season in your life or family? God did not promise that the way would be easy. Oftentimes, God's ways are harder than the ways of the world. But He did promise that He will be with you always.

Don't give up on God. He certainly has not given up on you! He will never turn His back on you or walk away from you. God will fulfill His promises, no matter how challenging the problem may be. As a matter of fact, problems and promises go hand in hand. If you want to be a person of great faith, then you have to be a person who sees past the problem to the promise. In other words, you must stop talking to God about your problems and start talking to your problems about God! Then start praising God for the answer! I think of Papa Wade, who pastored all those churches long ago. Although he could see down the road only part of the way, in his spirit he envisioned generations of churches, congregations, and family members who would serve God. Because of his example, we have a family full of pastors, pastors' wives, deacons, musicians, writers, prayer warriors, and worshipers who love and serve God.

I want it to go on record that I believe God. And I'm standing on 2 Timothy 1:12: "I know whom I have believed, and am persuaded that he is able to keep that which I have committed unto him against that day." Will you go on record with me? Are there generations of believers in your family, just as there are in mine? Then we have the joy of knowing that we are continuing a precious spiritual heritage of faith for those who come behind us. Does your family's spiritual heritage begin with you or your generation? Then you have laid the groundwork for a godly legacy in your family that will continue for generations to come. As you believe God today, remember that faith without works is not really faith at all. If He says, "Go," step out in faith and trust Him to do a wonderful work in you and through you. This I know for sure: God has never, ever turned His back on people who believed Him, and He won't leave you either.

CHAPTER 12

THE POWER OF FAITH

If anyone is in Christ, that person is part of the new creation. The old
things have gone away, and look, new things have arrived!
—*2 Corinthians 5:17 CEB*

A rich life is measured not by the quantity of dollars in one's bank account but by the quality of one's relationships. No amount of money can compare to the joy that comes when we connect with others. And nothing can bring more comfort in a difficult season than a good friend. Relationships make life meaningful and enjoyable, especially relationships central to our existence—those with parents, siblings, spouses, children, and friends. There is real joy to be found when you know there are people who really care about you and believe in you.

After more than thirty-three years of marriage and ministry, my greatest support is still my husband, Charles. We have traveled all over the world together—from the Windy City to the City of Lights; from the concrete jungles in urban centers of America to the dusty roads and lush jungles of Africa. Charles is the quintessential roadie and residential song critic. Bless his heart, he has heard some of the songs in my repertoire again and again for almost as long as we have been married, and he often responds to those same songs as if he is hearing them for the first time. He assures me that of all the singers he enjoys, he considers me his favorite.

My life is also richly blessed by my two sons, great musicians in their own right. They are singers, composers, performers, music producers, and audio engineers. Now that they are adults with careers of their own, I'm no longer their teacher but their student. We've had the privilege to work together on stage and in the studio, on music projects and recordings, and nothing thrills my heart more than for one of them to pat me on the back and say, "You did a great job, Mom!" There is no greater joy as a wife and mother than finding ways to support and bless my family. In a family relationship, you shouldn't have to perform or do anything to impress others. You can just be yourself. Family should be a place where you are celebrated, not just tolerated.

I am awed that almighty God wants us to be His friends and a part of His family. It is mind-boggling to think that a holy God would want to befriend and belong to unholy people. He was the initiator in this relationship, loving us first, pursuing us relentlessly, drawing us to Him, giving us

His name. And because of Jesus, we are in right standing with God. We are holy, as He is holy. While other religions are perpetuated by fear, duty, obligation, and ritual, a Christian's relationship with Jesus is characterized by an intimate relationship with Him and the deep love that grows as a result. As Lord and Master, Jesus does not drive us as worthless slaves but draws us as precious friends.

AN UNLIKELY ALLY

Every family is made up of a variety of unique and colorful family members. Some are commended for their virtues; others are condemned for their vices. The family of God is no different. We are all unlikely characters, from all occupations and walks of life. We are a family of men and women, each with a story of how we were once dead in sin, but God's grace and mercy brought us to life in Him. And if you place your life completely in His hands, He'll give you a place to serve Him and a testimony that will give His name glory in the earth.

The Bible gives us interesting details concerning one of those unlikely people God used thousands of years ago, and we are still talking about her today. Rahab the harlot was a woman of questionable moral character in an unsavory occupation. Her story is told in Joshua 2. Let's start reading at verse 1: "Joshua, the son of Nun sent out of Shittim two men to spy secretly, saying, Go view the land, even Jericho. And they went, and came into an harlot's house, named Rahab, and lodged there."

Her home, which she also used as her place of business, was a part of the city wall of Jericho. Some scholars describe her as a savvy businesswoman who seized an opportunity to make a decent living. No matter how acceptable to the culture of the day her occupation may have been, the Bible still refers to her as a harlot—a common prostitute. The two men that Joshua sent to survey the land certainly did not seek Rahab for her occupation but for her location. Her home was built right into the city wall. This position was significant because many men who traveled through the city found accommodations in Rahab's home, and wherever men gather, they talk. Even today, it's commonplace to see men gathered around the lunch table at the local restaurant, discussing politics, sports, religion, and the state of the economy.

Over the years, Rahab had heard the stories of the God of the Israelites: His power to deliver His people, slay their enemies, and conquer kings and kingdoms on behalf of His chosen people. She also knew that all of Jericho was terrified of the Israelites. God strategically used Rahab the harlot—an unlikely heroine—to save the lives of two Israelite spies and help the Israelites journey to the Promised Land.

Now I'm going to ask you a question, and I want you to give it a bit of thought. Of all the people you know, who is the one person you can think of living a life that is far away from the Lord right now? Can you think of someone who, in your opinion, is making a mess of his or her life? Maybe he lives on the wrong side of the tracks and, for a lot of reasons, doesn't stand a chance. Maybe she's involved in a questionable practice like prostitution or drugs. Does the name or face of someone you love come across your mind? Maybe it's a husband who has packed up and left. Maybe it's a daughter who is out on the street. It could be someone who does not know Jesus as Savior.

It's easy to give up and write off that person, thinking that he or she is a lost cause. But in God's family there are no lost causes. No mistake is too offensive. No relationship is ever hopeless. No family member is worthy of giving up on. No life is worthy of being kicked to the curb. Rahab the harlot is proof of that. And if you're honest, as I'm being honest here, you can look at your life and thank God that He never gave up on you either.

A LIFE TRANSFORMED

For forty long and tedious years, the Israelite nation had wandered through the wilderness. Moses, their leader, had died, and they were under the capable leadership of Joshua, a faithful and courageous man. Joshua knew that in order for God's people to occupy the Promised Land, they had to take the city of Jericho, so he sent his spies to get the lay of the land. Let's continue to read from Joshua 2:

> Someone told the king of Jericho, "Men from the Israelites have come here tonight to spy on the land." So the king of Jericho sent word to Rahab: "Send out the men who came to you, the ones who came to your house, because they have come to spy on the entire land. But [Rahab] had taken the two men and hidden them. Then she said, "Of course the men came to me. But I didn't know where they were from. The men left when it was time to close the gate at dark, but I don't know where the men went. Hurry! Chase after them! You might catch up with them." But she had taken them up to the roof and hidden them under the flax stalks that she had laid out on the roof.
>
> (vv. 2-6 CEB)

Now Rahab was an insightful woman. She had heard all the things being said about the God of Israel. This Canaanite woman, who lived among a pagan people, was not just a good listener. She understood that the God of Israel was like no other god in history. Although she had only heard about these great exploits God had performed on behalf of His people, she did what every believer must do: she accepted what she heard by faith, believing that the God of the Israelites existed and had power. So she decided to help the two enemy spies. Believing Jericho would inevitably be conquered by the Israelites, she made up her mind that when the walls came tumblin' down to be on the Lord's side.

Yet no matter how noble and courageous her reactions were, Rahab's response to God was not perfect. She lied to protect the two Israelite spies. We cannot excuse her behavior, even though it was for a good cause that saved lives. God's commandments are explicitly clear that lying is never an acceptable practice (Leviticus 19:11; Colossians 3:9). She is to be commended for her acts of courage but not for her action of being dishonest. Rahab had developed a heart for God, but she was not yet acquainted with His laws. It could be that she did not quite understand all the implications of the life she had led, but she knew one thing for sure—the God of Israel was the God she would serve for the rest of her life. And it's just like God to use her life and even her lifestyle to bring her to a place of repentance and complete dedication to Him. The Bible tells us that the kindness of the Lord leads us to repentance (Romans 2:4). In her heart, she sensed the Lord drawing her, and she responded.

Rahab is a vivid example of what God can do when a person turns her heart and life over to Him. God is so good at taking the worst in us and using that very thing to bring out the best in us. Here is a woman who ended up putting everything on the line for God and His people. Rahab possessed courage and conviction that could come only from God. She was able to look impending doom, even death, squarely in the eye and decide that she would not be a victim of certain disaster but be used as a key to certain victory for God's people.

Because of Rahab's actions, the Israelites defeated the people of Jericho and received Rahab and her family into the nation of Israel. Rahab would learn the laws of God, maturing in her faith, and the transformation that came to this Canaanite prostitute is indicative of the fact that God can transform any life that is completely yielded to Him. Here is the proof: Rahab married Salmon, the son of a prominent leader among the tribes. Their son Boaz was one of the most faithful men who ever lived. Boaz married Ruth, and they had a son named Obed, who was the father of Jesse, whose son was King David. And from the lineage of King David came Jesus Christ, the Savior of the world. And Rahab, along with Abraham's wife, Sarah, are the only two women mentioned in the Hall of Faith in Hebrews 11.

Only God could take a woman from such a common beginning to a place of such high esteem. What a miracle. What a heritage. What a God!

GOD CAN USE ANYONE

Never forget that God can use the most ordinary person to do the most extraordinary things. When it comes to the most unlikely people used by God, Charles and I are at the front of the line. When I was a young Christian, still singing and playing the piano for my father's church, I compromised my walk with the Lord by singing for the world in bars and clubs. My heart was divided, and I was looking for love in all the wrong places. But Jesus changed my life from the inside out. And when Charles made the Lord Jesus his Savior many years ago, he became a brand-new man from the inside out. If it had not been for the Lord, who was on our side, who knows where we would be. We'll be the first to tell you that apart from Jesus, everything about us is a disaster waiting to happen. But God, in all His grace, chooses to use us in spite of our shortcomings.

Charles loves the nations of Africa, and on one of his missionary trips to Uganda, he was the only layperson in the group along with six pastors. One Sunday morning each pastor was given a preaching assignment at a church throughout the city. Much to Charles's surprise, he was given a preaching assignment too. He protested, "I don't think so! I'm nobody's preacher. Don't expect *me* to get up before a congregation and deliver a sermon!" But the arrangements had already been made, and there was no getting out of it.

That morning Charles shared his testimony of how he came to know the Lord Jesus as Savior. Many hearts and lives were touched and changed as a result. Later that week, Charles and all of the pastors were meeting with the men in a nearby village for Bible study on marriage and family. During the lunch break, one of the African men approached Charles and asked if he could speak with him. The man told Charles something he was not expecting. The man had accepted Christ the Sunday before and expressed his desire to live a life that was pleasing to Christ. But, the man told Charles, he had seven wives. As a result, he had seven families and more than twenty-five children to care for. He presented his dilemma to Charles, wondering what he should do: "Do I divorce six wives and choose only one? Do I divorce them all and start all over again? What do I do?" Charles swallowed hard, sending up a silent prayer before giving the man his answer.

The answer Charles gave is simply amazing to me. Charles

said this to the man with seven wives: "You can't undo what you've already done. You made the choice to marry those women, and now, what's done is done. You must continue to support and take care of them. You're going to have to live with the consequences of your choices. But from now on you must teach your children that God commands that men are to have only one wife, and women are to have only one husband."

Only God could have imparted that wisdom to Charles at a moment when he needed it most. You see, my good friend, there is a problem somewhere just waiting for you to fix. There is a dilemma out there right now that needs solving, and you hold the key. I hope by now, after reading this far into this book, you're not the least bit tempted to say, "Well, I'm not qualified to do anything for God." I pray that you're not thinking, *Why, God could* never *use me to accomplish anything.* No, dear one, I hope by now you know that you know for sure, God doesn't call the qualified; He qualifies the called.

There are all kinds of people in the family of God. Everyone has a story that testifies to the love and amazing grace of God: "The old life is gone; a new life has begun!" (2 Corinthians 5:17 NLT). I hope that you can trust God to use every aspect of your life story, and you can say this along with me, "This I know for sure: I'm not all that I want to be. And I'm not all I'm going to be. But praise God, I'm not all I used to be!"

THERE IS A GOD IN HEAVEN
AND I AM IN HIS PLAN
HE WILL FORSAKE ME NEVER
MY LIFE IS IN HIS HANDS

His boundless love will lead me
As long as time endures

Oh, this I know
This I know for sure

Lord, with glowing heart I'd praise thee
For the bliss thy love bestows,
For the pardoning grace that saves me,
And the peace that from it flows:
Help, O God, my weak endeavor;
This dull soul to rapture raise;
Thou must light the flame, or never
Can my love be warmed to praise.

Praise, my soul, the God that sought thee,
Wretched wanderer, far astray,
Found thee lost, and kindly brought thee
From the paths of death away;
Praise, with love's devoutest feeling,
Him who saw thy guilt-born fear,
And, the light of hope revealing,
Bade the blood-stained cross appear.

Lord, this bosom's ardent feeling
Vainly would my lips express;
Low before thy footstool kneeling,
Deign thy suppliant's prayer to bless.
Let thy grace, my soul's chief treasure,
Love's pure flame within me raise,
And, since words can never measure,
Let my life show forth, thy praise.

—Francis Scott Key[1]

CHAPTER 13

THE GOD WHO RELENTLESSLY LOVES

I will be in them and you will be in me so that they will be completely
one. Then the world will know that you sent me and that you loved them
just as much as you loved me.
—John 17:23 NCV

It was a landmark moment for me the day I realized how much God really loves me. I've heard the words "God loves you" all my life, but one morning while I was reading John 17:23, the words seemed to leap off the page and into my heart.

Jesus was praying for His disciples as well as for those who would believe their message. In amazement, I realized that because I am a believer, Jesus was praying for *me* as He spoke to His Father—our Father—in heaven.

The weight of His words came alive with understanding for me that day. Has this ever happened to you? You've read a certain passage from God's word many times. You're familiar with it. You've underlined it in your Bible and highlighted it with a neon-colored marker. You've made notes in the margin of your Bible. You've memorized it, and you've given yourself a gold star and a pat on the back for a job well done. Then one day you read it again, and somehow the words take on a new dimension. They come alive as if you were reading them for the very first time.

That's what happened to me that day when I read John 17:23. I had read those words in the past, but that day they touched my heart like never before. Even now, I'm overwhelmed with awe at the thought of it: "Then the world will know that you sent me and that *you loved them just as much as you loved me*" (John 17:23 NCV, emphasis mine). I thought, *God, You love me just as much as You love Jesus? That's incredible! That's way too much for my mind to take in. You—the God of the universe—love me like that? With all my faults? After everything I've done? You love me as much as You love Your holy, blameless Son?* What kind of love goes to such an extent?

LOVE'S AUDACITY

The word of God is not only life-changing; it's life-giving. It's true that the Bible is the only book you can read and never finish. You will discover a fresh revelation every time you open the word of God. Have you ever tasted freshly baked bread straight from the oven? Just thinking about it might cause you to imagine how good fresh bread can be. The word of God is always fresh—no stale, leftover blessings for us. Jesus said, "I am the bread of life: he that cometh to me shall never hunger" (John 6:35).

What about thirst? Have you ever had your thirst quenched by a long drink from a tall glass of cool water on a hot summer day? The word of God is more refreshing than that. Jesus added, "He that believeth on me shall never thirst" (John 6:35). The Bible is the living word of God. It is alive with meaning, potential, and power. Like a scalpel in the hands of a skilled surgeon, God's word has the power to convict us of sin, eliminating anything that is not like Christ. Our lives are laid open before the only One who has the ability to penetrate the hardest of hearts, reveal any faults, and show us the way we should live. Every word has the potential to heal the sick, bring sight to the blind, comfort the lonely, add joy to the brokenhearted, and bring understanding to those who long for insight: "The word of God is quick, and powerful, and sharper than any twoedged sword" (Hebrews 4:12).

That morning while I was sitting at the breakfast table with a cup of coffee and my Bible, the word of God quickened my heart, and I haven't been the same since. Why? I discovered that God loves me as if I were the only one to love.

It's true for you as well! God loves you just as much as He loves His own Son. You see, He not only loves you; He is *in* love with you. The Lord declared, "Yea, I have loved thee with an everlasting love: therefore, with lovingkindness have I drawn thee" (Jeremiah 31:3). Listen to how *THE MESSAGE* states this promise: "I've never quit loving you and never will. / Expect love, love, and more love!" He takes great pleasure in you and delights in finding ways to demonstrate His love toward you.

God loves you as if you were His only child. His attention is never divided, nor is He ever distracted. His eyes are always on you. I like to say it like this: "You're God's favorite." When I first heard that phrase, "I'm God's favorite," I tripped over the words. I could hardly get the expression out of my mouth that Sunday when our pastor asked us to exchange the words with the person sitting next to us. I said the phrase but with a great deal of hesitation. I felt that making that bold statement was overstepping a boundary, giving myself way too much credit.

Maybe you, too, are having a difficult time wrapping your mind around such a thought. Maybe you're thinking, *How could I be God's favorite? I've got issues. I have a past filled with dreadful mistakes. I've broken promises, and I've let God down. How could God love me like that?* God does not give preferential treatment to some of us while treating others like second-class citizens. He doesn't play favorites. That's not the meaning here. As I've searched God's word, this is what I've found: God does not accept you based on your righteousness. No matter how hard you try to be good, you will fall short. On your own, you will never measure up. You're not God's favorite because of who you are: "We are all as an unclean thing, and all our righteousnesses are as filthy rags" (Isaiah 64:6). You are not God's favorite because of anything you have done: "All have sinned, and come short of the glory of God" (Romans 3:23).

You are God's favorite because of what Jesus did for you on the cross at Calvary. I used to think, *I need to be a better Christian. I need to read the Bible more and pray more and go to church more. Be a better wife and mother.* Every one of those things is a worthy goal. But achieving worthy goals does not make me or you God's favorite. In your own strength, you could never qualify for such a position. But Jesus does qualify, and He qualified you. You are God's favorite because Jesus is God's favorite! The great work Jesus did at the cross satisfied the sacrifice for sin once and for all: "God's will was for us to be made holy by the sacrifice of the body of Jesus Christ, once for all time" (Hebrews 10:10 NLT). You don't have to work to earn God's love. You *can't* work for it; it's a gift.

LOVE'S GENEROSITY

One day a friend dropped by our home for a short visit. A thoughtful person, she came bearing gifts—a jar of local honey from a beekeeper's farm right up the road to share with Charles and a beautiful bouquet of flowers in autumn colors for me. Surprised, elated, and grateful, I hugged her neck, thanked her, put the bouquet in a pretty vase, and placed it at the center of the kitchen table. We chatted while I put on the kettle for tea. Soon we were enjoying each other's company, sipping hot tea sweetened with the honey she brought.

After a little bit, she left, but I was able to enjoy the results of her visit for several days. The flowers brightened up the house and brought a smile to my face each time I came through the kitchen. The honey lasted for a long time after that. Sometimes I'd put it in tea or mix it with a squirt of lemon juice right on the spoon to soothe my throat after a day when I'd used my voice a little too much. I thought about the generous spirit in which she shared her gift and how a simple heartfelt gesture could have such lasting impact.

Then I thought about the whole gift-giving process. That someone would think enough of me to take time and make the effort to bring me a gift was humbling. No matter how simple or elaborate a gift, the process shows sacrifice on behalf of the giver. In many instances, the act of giving far outshines the actual gift. How rude it would have been had I said to my friend on the day she visited, "Oh no. You shouldn't have. Please take these things back! I don't deserve them." I thought about how insulting it would have been for me to say, "Let me pay you for these things. Wait right here while I write you a check."

It's true. I didn't deserve the gifts. But gifts are never deserved. You can't earn a gift. A gift is bestowed. She wanted to bless me. She knew it would make me happy. The moment I saw the gift bag leave her hands, I got excited. I love gifts! I anticipated what was inside the beautiful presentation of her gift bag, decked with colorful paper billowing out of the top and curly streamers cascading down the side. Words of thanks came out of my mouth before I could even reveal the contents. I was so happy to be a recipient, grateful that she thought of me. She was excited to give the gift, and I was excited to be on the receiving end of her generosity.

Dear friend, in the same way, salvation in Jesus Christ is a gift: "It is by grace you have been saved, through faith—and this is not from yourselves, it is the gift of God—not by works, so that no man can boast" (Ephesians 2:8-9 NIV). There is no way you could ever do enough or be good enough to earn God's love. No matter how hard you try, you could never repay Jesus for all He has done for you. You can never pray enough. Or go to church enough. Or do enough good deeds. You may as well stop trying. Hallelujah! Jesus has done enough! Listen to what Romans 5:8 tells us: "God commendeth his love toward us, in that, while we were yet sinners, Christ died for us."

God granted you the Gift of all gifts—the gift of His Son. I love what THE MESSAGE says in that same passage: "We can understand someone dying for a person worth dying for, and we can understand how someone good and noble could inspire us to selfless sacrifice. But God put His love on the line for us by offering his Son in sacrificial death while we were of no use whatever to him." Your response is to receive the gift of salvation with a heart of gratitude and praise. The gift of God's love and favor is yours with no strings attached! Salvation is free, but it was not cheap. It cost Jesus His life through death on a cross. Romans 6:23 reminds us: "For the wages of sin is death, but the free gift of God is eternal life in Christ Jesus our Lord" (ESV). The only appropriate response is to say, "Thank You, Jesus," in words and deeds by living a life that overflows with gratitude for all that Jesus has done.

You see, to be God's favorite means you don't get what *you* deserve. You get what *Jesus* deserves. You deserve death. But because you are loved with an everlasting love, you receive eternal life. You are not God's favorite because of who *you* are. You are God's favorite because of *whose* you are.

LOVE'S IDENTITY

There is a sermon illustration about the renowned artist Paul Gustave Doré (1821–83) losing his passport while on a tour in Europe. When he came to a border crossing, he explained his predicament to one of the guards. Giving his name to the official, Doré hoped that he would be recognized and allowed to pass. The guard explained that many people attempted to cross the border by claiming to be people they were not. Doré insisted that he was who he claimed to be.

"All right," the border guard replied. "We'll give you a test, and if you pass it, we'll allow you to go through." Then the guard told the artist to sketch several peasants who were standing nearby.

Doré pulled out his notebook and did it so quickly and so skillfully that the guard was convinced he was indeed who he claimed to be. His work confirmed his word.

Christ's work confirms His word. And His word is at work in you every day as you are being shaped and molded into His image. Your identity is in Him. You are to look like Him in every way. You are to walk like Him and talk like Him. Love like Him and serve like Him. Your identity is not in who people say you are. Your identity is in who Jesus says you are. Listen to His words in Matthew 5:48: "You're kingdom subjects. Now live like it. Live out your God-created identity. Live generously and graciously toward others, the way God lives toward you" (THE MESSAGE). What Jesus says about you in His word is all that matters. Television, magazines, and Hollywood movies deliver the message that to be loved and accepted, to be considered beautiful, you have to look a certain way, be a certain age, have a certain body size, or acquire certain possessions. But you must not define yourself according to the world's standards.

The other day while standing in the grocery store checkout lane, I glanced at the magazine covers propped up in the stands. They displayed pictures of some of Hollywood's biggest sensations. The women were young, white, thin, and blonde. Let me say, I'm not mad at any of those women. They deserve accolades for their accomplishments, and I applaud their efforts. In some cases, I can say that I appreciate their work. But if I were taking my cues from the messages delivered by the media, I'd never fit in! I'm an older African American grandmother with hips! Sometimes I showcase my own naturally curly hair. Sometimes I put my hair on in the morning and take it off at night. No shame in my game. I'm happy just being me. And you have to be happy just being you! Don't fall for the subtle, alluring message of our culture: "Blend in; conform to the latest trend; copy the crowd. If you want to be beautiful and successful, buy this product. Try this diet and be the perfect size. Wear this fashion accessory."

I'm not saying that outward appearances aren't important. Not at all. But like a stained-glass window, your true beauty is best revealed by the light that shines through your life. You were never meant to blend in. You are at your best when you stand out! The Apostle Paul spoke very powerful words in Romans 12:1-2. This passage bears repeating, so read it with intention:

> So here's what I want you to do, God helping you: Take your everyday, ordinary life—your sleeping, eating, going-to-work, and walking-around life—and place it before God as an offering. Embracing what God does for you is the best thing you can do for him. Don't become so well-adjusted to your culture that you fit into it without even thinking. Instead, fix your attention on God. You'll be changed from the inside out. Readily recognize what he wants from you, and quickly respond to it. Unlike the culture around you, always dragging you down to its level of immaturity, God brings the best out of you, develops well-formed maturity in you. (*THE MESSAGE*)

You see, you're way past different. You're unique. You're one of a kind in your distinction. You're in a class all by yourself. There's nobody else like you on the planet. No, let me rephrase that. There is nobody like you in the entire universe. Jesus celebrates you! Celebrate your uniqueness by giving God glory for making you just the way He wanted. Don't waste your time trying to be someone else. If you are busy trying to be someone else, you will leave a huge void in the world where the real you ought to be.

It all begins and ends with His great love for you. Regardless of who you are or how far you have fallen, God's unfaltering love will reach to wherever you are. No matter how deeply you've been wounded or how badly it hurts, God's love is just the prescription you need for what ails you.

No matter who has rejected you, God has already placed His stamp of approval on your life. This is what God's word says about you: "He made us accepted in the Beloved" (Ephesians 1:6 NKJV™).

Don't think you're beautiful? Think again. If God says you're beautiful, that settles the matter: "Let the king be enthralled by your beauty; / honor him, for he is your lord" (Psalm 45:11 NIV).

Need a really good friend? You've found one in Jesus: "There is a friend who sticks closer than a brother" (Proverbs 18:24 NIV).

Been rejected? Not anymore! Our loving Lord also said, "Whoever comes to me I will never drive away" (John 6:37 NIV).

Think you're too bad to be forgiven? Never in a million, trillion, gazillion years. Believe these words of John: "If we confess our sins, he is faithful and just to forgive us our sins and to cleanse us from all unrighteousness" (1 John 1:9).

LOVE'S AUTHENTICITY

You are God's favorite. He loves you as if you were an only child. You are His very own. Let me ask you this: What do you call the people who occupied the land of Canaan? The Canaanites, right? What do you call those who inhabited the land of Moab? The Moabites, yes? And what do you call the people who lived in the land of Israel? The Israelites, correct? Because you are a recipient of God's great love, because you occupy the land of His wonderful favor, what are you called? You are called a Favorite! You are His—a member of His forever family, a chosen people, a holy nation. His love is in you, upon you, and around you, and it works through you. When you realize how much you are loved by God, you become so filled up with His love and compassion that you want to share His love with others in your ordinary "walking-around" life. I don't know much, but one thing I do know for sure: God loves you as if you were the only one to love. He loves you just as much as He loves His own Son.

Do you believe that to the extent that you want to live it out? When you do, you can risk loving others to put love on the line. I've asked God to use me like that: however He wants and whenever He wants. One day He took me up on it. That day I was at the doctor's office to get my annual mammogram, and I was a bit anxious. Getting a mammogram is not one of my favorite things to do. The whole ordeal is uncomfortable, beginning with the gown the technician had given me to put on (which was less like a cotton gown and more like an oversized paper towel). And there's nothing I love better than having my teacups squeezed into saucers, if you know what I mean. But on an annual basis, I do what must be done.

I was waiting when I heard a soft knock at the door. Another nurse poked her head into the room. She had a smile on her face and a certain look in her eyes. She said, "Are you Babbie Mason?"

I sheepishly answered, "Uh . . . yeah?"

She exclaimed with delight: "I knew it! I knew that was you! I saw you at a Women of Faith Conference! Would you mind singing my favorite song, 'Standing in the Gap'?"

She was asking for my permission while calling other nurses into the room. Quickly, I literally tried to pull it together. I adjusted the paper towel gown around me a little more, as if it had more to give. (It had nothing more to give.) But I was about to give the concert of a lifetime. The room filled with nurses, technicians, and only the Lord knows who else. Without so much as an apology, I opened my mouth and sang to encourage the hearts of women along life's journey:

> I'll be standing in the gap for you
> Just remember someone, somewhere, is praying for you
> Calling out your name, praying for your strength
> I'll be standing in the gap for you.[2]

I looked into each face as I sang. An examining room became holy ground, and a paper towel gown became a choir robe. I learned that day that people everywhere are starved for love. They don't care what the setting looks like. If there's a fire in your heart, they will draw near it to keep warm. If you're serving something good to eat, they will gather around the table and pull up a chair. They don't even care how well you're dressed. Love is the best garment there is.

This I know for sure: you are God's favorite. Whether you are at home, at the mall, or on your job, share the love of Jesus in your sleeping, eating, going-to-work, and walking-around life.

CHAPTER 14

THE GOD WHO WILLINGLY FORGIVES

In all these things we are more than conquerors through him that loved us. For I am persuaded, that neither death, nor life, nor angels, nor principalities, nor powers, nor things present, nor things to come, nor height, nor depth, nor any other creature, shall be able to separate us from the love of God, which is in Christ Jesus our Lord.

—Romans 8:37-39

I've heard it said that self is in the root, the shoot, and the fruit of our human existence. And isn't that how sin starts? A selfish act starts as the seed of a thought, then it rises up on the inside. Before long it stands to its feet, flails its arms, and says, "I want it my way. I want it all and I want it *now!*" There is a selfish prodigal in all of us. We are not satisfied with the way things are, and we don't usually stop until we get our way.

People haven't changed much over the centuries, have we? When we look back through the Bible, we see that Adam and Eve got their way when they ate of the tree. David and Bathsheba got their way when they slept together outside marriage. Jacob got his way when he took advantage of his dysfunctional family. Judas got his way when he betrayed Jesus with a kiss. Peter wasn't satisfied until he denied Jesus three times.

In Luke 15, Jesus told the story of the prodigal son, sometimes known as the parable of the lost son. Jesus told us this parable to reveal the nature of the human heart and, more important, to show the true, loving nature of our God.

HAVE IT YOUR WAY

> He said, A certain man had two sons: and the younger of them said to his father, Father, give me the portion of goods that falleth to me. And he divideth unto them his living. And not many days after the younger son gathered all together, and took his journey into a far country, and there wasted his substance with riotous living. And when he had spent all, there arose a mighty famine in that land; and he began to be in want. (Luke 15:11-14)

The parable of the prodigal son is a story to which, unfortunately, many of us can relate. The account reveals the relationship between a father and his two sons. One day the restless younger son asked his father to go ahead and give him his share of his inheritance. For a Jewish son to ask this was an offense to his father because a son never receives his father's inheritance until after his father's death. So, in essence, the son was saying to his father, "I wish you were dead." But the son was insistent, and the father granted his desire.

When he got his money, the young man headed for a far-off country where he wasted his wealth on what Jesus called "riotous living." In other words, he spent all his money on good wine, pretty women, and wild living. It wasn't long before his money ran short, and he could no longer afford the lifestyle to which he had grown accustomed. Then his money ran out completely just as a severe famine plagued the land. When a person is desperate, he or she will do just about anything. And so it was with this nice Jewish boy. To earn a few pennies, he got a job feeding the pigs. He stooped so low that he not only touched unclean pigs but also was tempted to eat the food he was feeding them.

That is what sin will do. Sin will take you farther than you want to go. Sin will make you pay more than you want to pay. And sin will make you stay longer than you want to stay. *Matthew Henry's Concise Commentary on the Bible* explains the nature of the prodigal heart:

> A sinful state is a state of *departure* and *distance* from God. . . .
> A sinful state is a *spending* state. . . . Wilful sinners . . . misemploy their thoughts and all the powers of their souls, misspend their time and all their opportunities. . . .
> A sinful state is a *wanting* state. . . . Sinners want necessaries for their souls; they have neither food nor raiment for them, nor any provision for hereafter. . . .
> A sinful state is a *vile, servile* state. . . . The business of the devil's servants is to *make provision for the flesh, to fulfil the lusts thereof,* and that is no better than feeding . . . swine.[1]

That was where the prodigal found himself—in the hog pen with a hopeless heart, an empty belly, and nowhere to lay his head.

Has sin ever left you hopeless, empty, out in the cold? You didn't plan for it to turn out that way, but most of the time sin isn't planned. Maybe that's why we use the phrase "fall into sin." You're walking along, minding your own business, when you lose your footing, and the next thing you know, you're slip-sliding away. The devil is a strategist. He sets you up to destroy you. The evil one doesn't fight fair; he catches you off guard and moves in when you're not looking. Satan knows how to lay you low. Before you can get up off the mat, he takes full advantage of an opportunity to hit you with his best shot, and before you know it, you're saying something you shouldn't. You tell the lie. You take the drink. You sneak off to make the phone call. You fudge the numbers. You do it just this once. You watch the video. You lose control. You lose ground. You lose hope.

You might be in the fight of your life right now, friend, but I want you to know something. The devil may have won the battle, but he has not won the war. And you have been given a deadly weapon with which to fight him: "The weapons of our warfare are not carnal, but mighty through God to the pulling down of strong holds" (2 Corinthians 10:4). Good friend, are you persuaded that you are not left to fight this battle alone? You have the Word of God, who is Jesus, to fight your battles for you. Pray the Word! Sing praises using the Word, speak the Word of God to resist the enemy, and watch that devil flee!

This is no time to be casual. Go on the defensive. Put on the whole armor of God from head to toe. Don't hang in there on what you feel, but stand on what you know for sure. Stand on this: "In all these things we are more than conquerors through him that loved us. For I am persuaded, that neither death, nor life, nor angels, nor principalities, nor powers, nor things present, nor things to come, nor height, nor depth, nor any other creature, shall be able to separate us from the love of God, which is in Christ Jesus our Lord" (Romans 8:37-39).

THE HARD WAY

Like the lost son, you may have discovered that the road leading to the big city is lined with bright lights and tempting sights. However, when you take the same road that leads back home again, each step can be laden with regret. The lessons learned on the streets are usually learned the hard way.

When I was a junior in college, my dream was to go to a big state university near Detroit so I would be closer to Motown and closer to realizing my dream as a Motown singer. But there was no money to attend the big university. Instead, I was accepted at Spring Arbor College, a small Christian school not even twenty miles from home. The deal was sealed when I was awarded a music scholarship to go to school there. I thought, *I'll just get my teaching degree, and that will give me something to fall back on.*

But while I was making my plans, God was activating His. My heart was set on singing R&B music: the music of Aretha Franklin and Gladys Knight; Diana Ross and Roberta Flack. On Friday and Saturday nights, I tried my hand at singing in local bars and clubs around the state of Michigan, on college campuses, and in smoky hotel piano bars. Every Sunday morning, though, I'd show up to sing and play the piano at my father's church. I had one foot in the church and one foot in the world. Talk about a setup for a fall!

One afternoon in late autumn I decided to have lunch in the school snack bar. I ordered a hot cup of beef vegetable soup and sat down at a table. Snow was already on the ground, and the hot soup felt good going down. A friend came by to chat, and in a few minutes she was on her way and I went back to my lunch. But since the soup had been sitting there for a few minutes, it grew lukewarm. I noticed that the fat in the soup had formed an orange ring around the rim of the white Styrofoam cup it was served in. I took another spoonful, but the soup's lukewarm broth coagulated and rolled off the spoon. It actually made my stomach feel queasy.

At that moment, a passage of scripture came to my mind. I remembered it word for word, since I had memorized it from my youth. Found in the book of Revelation, it is written to the church at Laodicea. But that day, it was like the letter said, "Dear Babbie." It was as if Jesus Himself sat down and had lunch with me. The scripture declares, "I know your works. You are neither cold nor hot. I wish that you were either cold or hot. So because you are lukewarm, and neither hot nor cold, I'm about to spit you out of my mouth" (Revelation 3:15-16 CEB).

God got my attention that day. I knew He was speaking directly to me and the compromising way I was living. Like the prodigal son, I came to myself. I surrendered my heart to the Lord right there at the lunch table. At that moment, I gave Jesus my desires, my dreams, my uncertainties, and my fears about the future. I realized at that moment that I didn't need a record contract, a full concert schedule, or a band to back me up. What I needed was a restored relationship with Jesus.

It was a landmark moment in the prodigal's life when he realized what he had left back at his father's house was better than what he faced out on the streets: "When he came to himself, he said, How many hired servants of my father's have bread enough and to spare, and I perish with hunger! I will arise and go to my father, and will say unto him, Father, I have sinned against heaven, and before thee, and am no more worthy to be called thy son: make me as one of thy hired servants" (Luke 15:17-19). Verse 20 adds, "He arose, and came to his father."

"When he came to himself . . ." What a powerful phrase! Have you ever come to yourself? You see, until you come to yourself you'll keep getting what you've always gotten. You'll continue to do what you have always done. When you come to yourself, you'll have one of those soul-searching conversations with yourself that may go something like this:

"I'm sick and tired of having too much month and not enough money." That's when you start getting out of debt.

"I can't take this anymore." That's when you decide to get help for your addiction.

"I can do bad all by myself." That's when you change the circumstances concerning the relationship that's gone south.

"I know I can do it." That's the moment you decide to take the first step toward launching your business or furthering your education.

The son came to himself. He got up from the pigpen and made the decision to go home. As the wayward son rounded the bend near home, he saw the familiar sites he had only dreamed of for so long. He recognized the hills that ran behind his father's home. He smelled the aroma of freshly cut hay. At first, reluctance and regret caused his gait to be slow and deliberate. His mind played tricks on him. Could he have wondered, *What will my father say? What will he do? Turn his back on me? Make me like one of his hired servants? Serves me right if my father never speaks to me again. Anything is better than where I've been.* Then who did he see coming up the road to meet him? Whose arms couldn't wait to embrace him?

With a heart full of love, overflowing with mercy, his father sprinted barefoot, completely leaving his sandals in the dust, robes hiked high and blowing in the breeze: "When he was yet a great way off, his father saw him, and had compassion, and ran, and fell on his neck, and kissed him" (v. 20).

I don't believe his father glanced up just in time to catch a glimpse of his son out of the corner of his eye. No, I believe his father had surveyed the horizon, day after painstaking day, hoping any moment to see his son come down the road. I believe he sat by the window each night keeping vigil until well after bedtime, then leaving a light on just in case his son came home in the middle of the night. Then the day came. When the son was down the road a way off, road weary, gaunt, and smelling like the hog pen, his father recognized even the slightest form of his son's silhouette and *ran* to meet him. In a state of disbelief, the young man collapsed into his father's arms, embraced, kissed by grace and mercy. No I told you so's. No sermon. Only a ring, a robe, and a party.

THE WAY OF LOVE

Evan Roberts was an uneducated coal miner from the country of Wales. At the turn of the twentieth century, God used this common workingman to spark the Welsh revival that eventually spread across the British Isles. Evan Roberts's preaching convicted the hearts and lives of all who heard him, at times leading entire congregations to salvation. The revival was so strong that taverns went into bankruptcy and closed. Dance halls struggled to stay open. The church was filled to overflowing, while attendance at football games slacked off. Jails emptied as crime fell. Courtrooms had no cases. Because the police had little to do, they formed a choir that sang at the daily meetings.

The inspiring hymn "Here Is Love," written by William Rees (1802–83), was sung during the days of the Welsh revival and has been a beloved hymn ever since. The words of the hymn celebrate the truth that repentance is generated not only by one's acknowledgment of sin or fear of hell but also by the wonderful love of Jesus Christ and His compassion for lost sinners. As you read these lyrics, allow them to speak to your heart:

Here is love, vast as the ocean,
Lovingkindness as the flood,
When the Prince of Life, our Ransom,
Shed for us His precious blood.
Who His love will not remember?
Who can cease to sing His praise?
He can never be forgotten,
Throughout Heav'n's eternal days.

On the mount of crucifixion,
Fountains opened deep and wide;
Through the floodgates of God's mercy
Flowed a vast and gracious tide.
Grace and love, like mighty rivers,
Poured incessant from above,
And Heav'n's peace and perfect justice
Kissed a guilty world in love.[2]

This is for certain: the names in the story may change. The faces in the story may be different. But it's the same story. Every one of us has defied our Father's wishes. We've all broken His heart. Each of us has wandered far from home and found ourselves in a faraway place, wallowing in the mire of sin. But no matter how far you roam, you are never too far from the reaches of God's grace. Jesus is the same today as He was back then. People were touched that day long ago when Jesus told the parable of the lost son, and lives continue to be changed by His words even today. I can tell you that His forgiveness was extended and gladly received by a young female college student at the lunch table more than thirty-five years ago. And I believe that He's calling you right now: "If we confess our sins, he is faithful and just to forgive us our sins, and to cleanse us from all unrighteousness" (1 John 1:9). The very moment you confess your sin and turn to Him, He is right there—ready, willing, and able to forgive.

Luke 15 is not only the story of the prodigal son. More appropriately, it is the story of our Father, the father of prodigals, who continues to astonish us with His extravagant display of abundant love. Don't deny yourself for another moment the joy of knowing you are forgiven and restored. You see, the Father withholds from you the very things you deserve—judgment and condemnation. And He extends to you the very things you *don't* deserve—grace and mercy.

Have you been running in the wrong direction? Do you think it's time that you turn around and look toward home? When you do, you will find that God has been there all along, waiting to receive you and lovingly restore you to your rightful place in His eternal family. Your loving Father has a royal robe and a signet ring that have been designed with you in mind, and He is waiting to clothe you with His choicest blessings. This I know for sure: the best is yet to come. He's thrown a party in your honor. What are you waiting for? Don't let the celebration begin without you!

CHAPTER 15

THE GOD WHO GOES OUT OF HIS WAY

*God so loved the world that he gave his only Son, so that everyone who
believes in him won't perish but will have eternal life.*
—John 3:16 CEB

I t was an exciting day. My friend, who had just produced her
first motion picture, had planned a big premiere at her home
church, and Charles and I were invited to come. On the way to
the church, I glanced at my watch and surmised that I still had
enough time to dash into a store to buy my friend a gift—maybe a bouquet of flowers—to celebrate her accomplishments.
Unfamiliar with the area, we could find only one of those big

warehouse-type superstores. It was the only choice we had at the moment, so Charles parked the car in the lot and waited while I dashed into the huge store.

I was a bit overwhelmed. The store seemed to stretch as far as it did wide. A nice store clerk pointed me in the direction of the fresh flowers. I thanked her, found a gift to go with the flowers, and was back at the front of the store in no time. I stepped into the checkout line, filing in behind two other people. The clerk told me I'd have to pay a bit extra because I didn't have a membership card. I'd never shopped at one of those warehouse superstores before, so I didn't know that a membership card was required. I was willing to pay a little extra for the gifts rather than spend time, effort, and gas looking for another store.

Just then, a nice middle-aged black lady behind me said, "No problem. I'll be glad to let you use my card so you can get the discount."

I replied with gratitude to her offer: "Oh, thank you so much! God bless you for that!"

"Oh, honey," she said, "I really do need God to bless me. I've had a tough go of it these last few months. My grandkids have come to live with me, and I'm not as young as I used to be. It's a challenge to raise kids nowadays."

In an effort to offer a simple word of encouragement, I smiled and said rather conversationally, "Well, may the Lord give you the strength you need to raise your grandkids. I pray He will open up the windows of His heaven and shower down so many blessings upon you and your grandchildren that you won't have room to receive them all."

That lady was catching the vision before I could get the words out of my mouth! The next thing I knew, she was lifting her hands and shouting praises to God, right there in the checkout line. "Praise You, God! Hallelujah! I receive that blessing right now, Jesus. Thank You, Lord, for blessing me!" she said.

I've been privileged to worship Jesus in a lot of different places, but that was the first time I'd ever had church in the checkout line of a warehouse superstore. Then, before I could turn around, a young lady standing behind us in line asked, "Will you bless me too?"

While the first lady was yet praising God, I smiled, took the young lady by the hand, and said to her, "Well, my sweet friend, God loves you so much! May you always live for the Lord. As you do, I pray that He will supply all your needs according to His riches in glory by Christ Jesus." The next thing I knew, tears came rolling down her face as she savored those words spoken into her life.

I paid for my items and was heading out the front door when the security guard standing at his post of duty asked, "If you don't mind, would you bless me too?"

The words I spoke to those I met that day at the store weren't exceptional. I only did what I was led to do—to encourage weary hearts through the power of the word of God. I marveled at how persuasive the spoken word of God is. I went into that store for one reason, but it was evident God sent me out of my way on a greater mission to minister His love to people who needed it most.

MAN ON A MISSION

Jesus spent His entire life and ministry going out of His way to bring others to Himself. As a matter of fact, that's what Jesus did best. Leaving the beautiful splendor of heaven, He consented to come all the way to earth so He could show us what love looks like in flesh and blood. The King of kings, He deserved a royal entourage to announce His arrival to earth. Instead, He chose to come into the world just like the rest of us—as a baby. And He was placed in a humble manger, a feeding trough for the animals. Instead of the wonderful fragrance of heaven, the first aroma He inhaled was the pungent odor of a stable filled with smelly farm animals.

That's what Jesus did and what He still does today. Jesus came to be the bridge between a holy God and a hopeless humanity so we could cross over from death to life. Jesus spoke the words the prophet Isaiah once said about Him:

> The Spirit of the Lord is on me,
>   because he has anointed me
>   to proclaim good news to the poor.
> He has sent me to proclaim freedom for the prisoners
>   and recovery of sight for the blind,
> to set the oppressed free,
>   to proclaim the year of the Lord's favor. (Luke 4:18-19 NIV)

That same Holy Spirit was upon my father, Pastor Willie G. Wade, who preached, Sunday in and Sunday out, to a mighty band of saints at Lily Missionary Baptist Church for almost forty years. The subject of the sermon didn't matter. Whether he preached on the power of faith or the sweetness of grace, the act of repentance or the authority of the name of Jesus, Dad always closed every sermon with the message of the gospel of Jesus Christ. And in that message, I can see clearly just how far Jesus had to come, how long Jesus had to reach, how wide His arms had to stretch, and how deep His love had to go to rescue us from the clutches of sin. Imagine my father preaching with that fiery, fervent passion black preachers of his generation are known for. Use your holy imagination, and picture my father, decked in his black preacher's robe, proclaiming the message of the gospel with every impassioned inflection of his voice:

> Jesus came down from heaven to earth, through forty and two generations. He caught Mary's nine-month train, He got off somewhere in Bethlehem, and there was no room for Him in the inn. The Word became flesh and dwelt among us. And we have seen His glory—the glory of the only begotten of the Father, full of grace and truth. Then they arrested Jesus and placed upon Him the sins of the whole world. They whipped Him all night long. They pierced Him in the side, gambled for His robe, nailed Him to an old rugged cross, and laid Him in a borrowed tomb. He went down in the grave on Friday. He stayed down in the grave on Saturday. But early . . . early . . . early on Sunday morning, the grave could no longer hold Him down. All power of heaven and earth is in His hands.

One day, at the age of thirty, Jesus took one last look around His earthly father's carpenter shop, shook the sawdust from His work apron, no doubt running his calloused hands across the wooden worktable where His hammer and nails waited to be put away. He kissed His mother good-bye and went about His heavenly Father's business. He walked the distance from Nazareth down to the Jordan River where John the Baptist was ministering to the crowds of people who had come to be baptized. And that day He *showed* the people as well as *told* the people of the importance of baptism. That day, Jesus, the Savior of the whole world, went out of His way to get in the line with sinners to be baptized. The Bible says, "When all the people were being baptized, Jesus was baptized too. And as he was praying, heaven was opened and the Holy Spirit descended on him . . . like a dove. And a voice came from heaven: 'You are my Son, whom I love; with you I am well pleased' " (Luke 3:21 NIV).

As the host of a television show called *Babbie's House*, I have the opportunity to meet many wonderful people who have beautiful testimonies of how Jesus delivered them from all manner of vices and destructive behaviors. I get to see the joy on their faces as they tell of how Jesus saved them from drug and alcohol abuse, prostitution, gambling, prison cells, and back alleys; how He healed their lives and restored families, marriages, and health. I've heard many of them say that they were still counting the days they have been clean. They were still excited about what Jesus had done in their lives, and they were still pressing on in the name of Jesus one day at a time.

If you have ever been washed in the blood of Jesus, you are as clean as you will ever be! If you have received Jesus as your Lord and Savior, you've been delivered from something that had the power to destroy your life. Are you still counting the days you've been clean before the Lord? If I live to see July 2013, I will have been clean—sin-free—fifty years! Now I know why they call that fifty-year anniversary the Year of Jubilee. It's the year to celebrate every sin forgiven, every debt canceled, and every hope restored! That's why, from time to time, the words of an old hymn rise up in my soul and I'm not satisfied until I sing them:

> Jesus paid it all,
> All to Him I owe;
> Sin had left a crimson stain,
> He washed it white as snow.
> —Elvina M. Hall, 1865

And now the Lord has put a new song in my mouth! I can't help singing about this confidence that celebrates how good He is. I wouldn't go back to that old life of doubt and insecurity for anything in the world, but I can look back for a moment and see where He's brought me from. Because I know that God is faithful and there is not a single variance in Him, I can trust

Him for whatever lies ahead. The last stanza of "This I Know for Sure" says,

So when my years are golden
The sun is sinking low
I'll not be moved by how I feel
But trust in what I know

JESUS GOES THE DISTANCE

Wherever Jesus went, He went out of His way to minister to the lost, the lonely, the sick, and the broken. Jesus went out of His way one day when He traveled through Samaria. He stopped to rest at Jacob's well that lazy, hazy day around noon. There He met a woman who had come to draw water. Jesus asked her for a drink. Her furrowed brow and sullen eyes told the painful story—the story of her life. She was a victim of her own circumstances. It was obvious that the burden the woman carried in her soul weighed more heavily upon her than the water pot she struggled to hoist upon her aching shoulders.

After five failed attempts at marriage, she had all but given up on love and had given in to living with a man who was not her husband, resigning herself to the fallacy that if you can't find what you need, just hold on to what you've got whether you want it or not. Relationships had stolen her dignity and self-worth one disappointment at a time until there was nothing left but a shell of a woman with little to show for her life but empty hopes and broken dreams. But she could see something different about this Man she met at the well. There was real love in His eyes. She could hear real hope in His voice. Real truth in His words. He said to her, "If you knew the gift of God and who it is that asks you for a drink, you would have asked him and he would have given you living water" (John 4:10 NIV).

That's what I love about Jesus. It doesn't matter who you are, where you've been, or how long you stayed, His love will draw you back from the brink of hopelessness and despair. He'd spoken to every parched place of this woman's heart, into every longing she'd had in her heart for years. Realizing that He was indeed the long-awaited Messiah, she dropped her water pot and went running back to the town to spread the news: "Come, see a man who told me everything I ever did" (John 4:29 NIV).

That's what Jesus did best. He went out of His way to speak life into those places in people's lives where death had already won. That was the situation when Jesus heard that His dear friend Lazarus had died. Jesus was delayed in getting back to Bethany, the very place where earlier the Jews had tried to stone Him, but He was compelled to travel the distance and brave His adversaries to go back and offer comfort to Lazarus's sisters, Mary and Martha, after the death of their brother.

Everything changed when Jesus came on the scene. He found Mary and Martha grieving and distraught over their loss. Jesus wiped His own tears and spoke to Lazarus, who was already decomposing in his grave: "Lazarus, come forth" (John 11:43). Only three words. Life conquered death. Let faith arise. Tears were dried. Death was defeated. Family was reunited. Sinners would believe.

No matter the distance, Jesus went—from big cities to small villages—healing people who could not walk, feeding the multitudes, giving sight to those who could not see, teaching in the Temple, raising the dead. He journeyed into the mountains, down by the river, to the garden, to the cross, to the grave, and back to prepare a place for us with Him in heaven.

HE WILL COME FOR YOU

James Whittaker was one of the seven crew members flying a famed B-17 Flying Fortress on a special mission during World War II. Captain Eddie Rickenbacker, a World War I flying ace and recipient of the Medal of Honor, was carrying a secret message for General Douglas MacArthur, and he was accompanied by an assistant. However, the plane was reported lost at sea in late October 1942. It encountered trouble with equipment after it flew out of radio range of Allied troops, and soon after that it ran out of gas somewhere over the Pacific and crashed into the ocean. The men spent the rest of October and much of November adrift in the ocean on rafts. They fought the heat of day, storms, and treacherous waves. Gigantic sharks, some as long as ten feet, rammed their nine-foot rafts, waiting for a meal. Within eight days, they had eaten the rations that had not been ruined by sea water. Their only hope for survival was a miracle.

One morning, following their daily devotions, Rickenbacker leaned his head back against the side of the raft and pulled his hat down over his eyes. Then he felt something land on his head. Peering out from under his hat, with every eager eye glued on him, he caught the seagull perched on his head, and the crew ate it. They used the bird's intestines for fish bait, and that provision allowed the crew to survive the ordeal to tell their story.

Just as in the story of the two fishes and five loaves to feed the multitude, God went to an unbelievable extent to provide for the stranded men until they were rescued. But that's not the real miracle. James Whittaker was not a believer. The plane crash didn't persuade him to give his life to Christ. All those days facing death on the open seas didn't cause him to think about eternity. In fact, Whittaker grew more and more irritated with John Bartek, a crew member who continually read his Bible audibly and privately.

But Bartek didn't stop reading, and the Holy Spirit didn't stop turning over the fallow ground of Whittaker's heart. Then came the moment the seagull landed on Captain Rickenbacker's head just after that morning's Bible reading. That was the moment James Whittaker became a believer.[1]

Only God would go to such extremes to capture one man's heart. It's just like God to send a winged missionary into the middle of nowhere to deliver a personal message of love and hope. Hearing that story brings new significance to John 3:16: "For God *so* loved the world, that he gave his only begotten Son, that whosoever believeth in him should not perish, but have everlasting life" (emphasis mine). God doesn't just love you; He *so* loves you. He loves you to an immeasurable extent. Jesus went the distance. And no matter how hard you try, you can't count that high or go that far.

Wherever you are at this very moment, whatever the condition of your heart, whatever your story, remember that Jesus wants you to be certain that He is at work in your life. In a warehouse superstore, in a little Baptist church on the east side of a Michigan town, by a well, by a tomb, on the open seas— the situation doesn't matter. The God of the universe wants you to always know for sure, beyond any shadow of doubt, that He is still going out of His way. And He will move heaven and earth for you.

PART SIX

THERE IS A GOD IN HEAVEN
AND I AM IN HIS PLAN
HE WILL FORSAKE ME NEVER
MY LIFE IS IN HIS HANDS
HIS BOUNDLESS LOVE WILL LEAD ME
AS LONG AS TIME ENDURES

Oh, this I know
This I know for sure

To thee, my righteous King and Lord,
My grateful soul I'll raise;
From day to day thy works record,
And ever sing thy praise.

Thy greatness human thought exceeds;
Thy glory knows no end;
The lasting record of thy deeds
Through ages shall descend.

Thy wondrous acts, thy power, and might,
My constant theme shall be;
That song shall be my soul's delight,
Which breathes in praise to thee.

The Lord is bountiful and kind,
His anger slow to move;
His tender mercies all shall find,
And all his goodness prove.

From all thy works, O Lord, shall spring
The sound of joy and praise;
Thy saints shall of thy glory sing,
And show the world thy ways.

Throughout all ages shall endure
Thine everlasting reign;
And thy dominion, firm and sure,
Forever shall remain.

—William Wrangham[1]

CHAPTER 16

WHEN YOU ARE SURE
OF WHAT YOU KNOW

By his divine power the Lord has given us everything we
need for life and godliness through the knowledge of
the one who called us by his own honor and glory.
—2 Peter 1:3 CEB

When I was seven, my Saturday mornings weren't complete until I had seen the weekly episode of *Mighty Mouse Playhouse*. A superhero in every sense of the word, that mouse could do anything! He could tunnel through concrete, stop a fountain of diesel fuel with one hand, and fix a car tire while the vehicle was speeding out of control—anything to keep Pearl Pureheart from meeting her fate at the hands of Oil Can Harry. In each episode, Pearl ended up in the hands of that dastardly cat, who inevitably tied the object of Mighty Mouse's affections to the railroad tracks. With the engine relentlessly hauling down the line in a rhythmic churn, Mighty Mouse swooped down, singing his famous line, " 'Here I come to save the day!' That means that Mighty Mouse is on the way!" In that unmistakable tenor voice, Mighty Mouse sang his way into Pearl's heart and mine when, at the last second, he delivered Pearl Pureheart and carried her off to live safely for another day.

Mighty Mouse was my champion in every way. Aside from the fact that he was a hopeless romantic *and* he could sing, he possessed an unbelievable amount of forethought, and he was kind, fearless, courageous, and dependable. No matter how many times poor Pearl fell into danger, you could count on him. Mighty Mouse would be right by her side to save her in an instant. Simply put, Mighty Mouse was the hero of every seven-year-old girl's dream. (And it is partially because of Mighty Mouse's influence and his beautiful tenor voice that I love the opera today.)

Sometimes faith and fiction can lead us to the same conclusion. Now, looking back on those episodes I loved as a child, I see a strong parallel between *Mighty Mouse Playhouse* and what it looks like to rely fully on God and take Him at His word.

I know now, that when you want to do great things, you will always have opposition. Expect it. Prepare for it. It's just a part of living. It's how you respond in the tough times and the tight spots that reveal what you're made of.

I know that there will always be scary moments and close calls—those moments when you see your life pass before your very eyes, and you marvel at how you made it through. One thing is certain, though. You'll never go through one of those difficult moments alone. Your Hero is only a call away.

I know now that we will meet people along life's journey who will need encouragement or a kind word. Do what you can to help them. They will be blessed and so will you.

Mighty Mouse taught me that life is packed full of adventure. There will be moments that steal your breath away and fill your heart with amazement. Don't miss the joy. You may have only one opportunity to savor that moment.

I've discovered that I may not know all the answers, but I will know what to do when the moment comes. And you'll recognize that moment even if there's barely enough light on the path to illuminate the next step.

One more lesson I remember now: there is always— always—a reason to sing. With the Hero by your side, you will be continually comforted by the sound of His voice and the familiar strains of His love song. Learn your part, and sing along. It is the sound of hope. It is the anthem of certain victory.

KNOWING GOD FOR WHO HE IS

It's easy for me to remember a cartoon character's attributes after so many years. What's more important is how vital it is for me to remember God's promises—not just for a year or a season, but for a lifetime. He's more faithful, kind, fearless, courageous, and dependable than any make-believe hero could ever be. Life *is* uncertain. But in those times of uncertainty, you must remember to rely on the truth you already know in your heart, then stand on what you know to be true regardless of how you may feel. The Lord knows what you're going through at this very moment, and He is orchestrating your circumstances for your good and His glory.

He does not want you to live your life in *reaction* to what you see and feel. He desires that you live your life in *response* to what He has already said. As you learn to trust Jesus for who He really is, you will find that is when your faith adventure really begins. The most successful way to establish trust for tomorrow is to get to know Jesus more intimately today.

My dear friend, thank you for going with me all the way to the end of this book! I wrote the song "This I Know for Sure," the song that inspired this book, to help you discover very important promises from the Lord. Now that we are here in these closing pages, my hope is that the words will be more than just a song; my hope is that they will be a prayer, a lifeline, that you can confidently hold on to in the days ahead. You see, the only things in this life that we can be absolutely sure of are those unchanging truths founded on God's eternal word. And when you determine that you will trust God's word no matter what, you realize God will take care of you *and* everything that concerns you.

For sure, you can trust God with every single detail of life. So the first question is: *What do you know for sure?* And the second: *How do you respond to what you know?* What you know for sure will establish the foundation upon which you build your life. To know perceptually, or in your mind, is one thing. But to know experientially, or in your heart, is where your faith must rest. And your response is directly determined by that foundation—the depth of your relationship with the Lord Jesus. It's not just what you know that matters. It's about *who* you know and how well you know Him that makes all the difference. Jesus, in His great power, will help you put what you know into practice. Peter reminded us, "By his divine power the Lord has given us everything we need for life and godliness through the knowledge of the one who called us by his own honor and glory" (2 Peter 1:3 CEB). As much as you want to know Him and grow in the knowledge of Christ, He wants you to know Him more.

No matter how well you think you already know Christ, you have the capacity to know Him in a deeper, more meaningful way. There is always room for a greater level of intimacy with Christ. This richer, fuller life is accessible to every believer. However, many Christians will never realize a more intimate walk with Jesus because they don't know or believe it's possible. It's like being presented with a beautiful gift, gorgeously wrapped and topped with a bow, but never opening it to reveal what's inside. Too many Christians have yet to discover that Jesus makes this rich and satisfying life available. And that, my friend, is a real tragedy. My prayer is that you will not miss out on anything that God has in store for you.

Be determined that you will open up your heart to receive the ways that Jesus wants to create this more intimate life with you. When you do, your life will reap wonderful rewards. You will see doubts vanish. You will realize a new level of faith. You will see the word of God come alive in your life. You will sense heartfelt compassion for those who are hurting. And you will experience a newfound excitement to share your faith with others. As we make ourselves available to God, there's no telling how He will use us to bring His love to the world!

That's what I've tried to convey in these pages as I've shared my personal stories and God-encounters with you. There is power in sharing what God has done for us, and I recommend that you tell your God-stories because, in doing so, we celebrate the fact that we are still here and God is still at work in our lives. Besides, now that I'm a grandmother, I've earned the right to repeat my stories as often as I see fit. So bear with me as I tell you about one more amazing thing the Lord has done.

It's the story of a young, tall, dark, and handsome African American soldier who made his way home after serving his country during World War II. This young man and his beautiful bride created a humble but loving home in the delta in the state of Mississippi. At that time in our nation's history, the South was in no way kind to black people, and this young couple had to endure economic hardship, the pains of prejudice and segregation, along with the day-to-day difficulties of being black in the Old South.

Not long after this young man arrived home, his wife received a letter from her parents, who had already migrated north during the early years of the second Industrial Revolution. In this letter, her mother encouraged them to leave the South and head north with the hopes of finding good jobs, nicer housing, better schools, overall a better life. This young couple did exactly that. They packed their meager belongings and their young son and headed north to Michigan.

The young man found a good job in one of the tire and rubber plants, but he remembered when he was a prisoner of war, held captive by the Germans. During his captivity, he cried out to God, and he promised the Lord that he would preach the gospel if the Lord would deliver him from his enemies. God was true to His word, and that young man was true to his. Soon he became the pastor of a fledgling ministry on the east side of a little town called Jackson. Their church family, filled with loving members, began to grow as their own family began to flourish. They had another son. Then their first daughter was born during the cold winter month of February.

Not long after the newborn girl was brought home from the hospital, tragedy struck when the young mother noticed that her baby's eyes did not focus well and the little one's head was beginning to swell. After examination, the doctor delivered the grim diagnosis that the child was hydrocephalic. In layman's terms, the disease is called "water on the brain." Surgery was immediately scheduled to place a shunt inside the child's skull to drain the cerebral fluid, hopefully alleviating the pressure on the brain. On the day of the operation, family and church members gathered in the waiting room to keep vigil while the surgeons prepared to perform the very delicate procedure in the surgery suite.

The doctors were hopeful but cautious because of the risks of the delicate surgery. But from the moment the surgical team made the first incision, they observed that the child's situation began to change. The pressure on her brain was beginning to ease, and the fluid around her brain was beginning to flow on its own. After further scrutiny, the doctors could find no reason to install the shunt, and they determined that the device would not be necessary. They credited medical advancements, but the prayer warriors in the family waiting room realized that they had been handed a miracle from the Lord. After several days in intensive care, the infant went home to lead a normal life.

A star student, she graduated from high school and college with honors. She entered the teaching profession, married a wonderful man, and started her own family. Later on, she ventured into a ministry that has taken her around the globe as a singer, songwriter, author, speaker, and TV talk show host who would have many opportunities to tell others of her love for Jesus.

That woman is *me*. I'm a living witness that God is a very faithful God. His faithfulness is not just something I heard about; this is something I know for myself. Satan tried to take me out, but Jesus said, "Hands off!" I know for sure that God has a plan for my life. And when you know you are in God's plan, you know nothing ever happens by chance. When He is in control of your life, nothing can come between you and God's great plan for you. Not people. Not things. Not slipups, setbacks, or near misses. Nothing can keep God's great plan for you from coming to pass.

KNOWING FOR SURE

Are you fearful or hesitant about the future? God wants you to have a stable mind and not live in fear: "God hath not given us the spirit of fear; but of power, and of love, and of a sound mind" (2 Timothy 1:7). "Behold, I am doing a new thing! Now it springs forth; do you not perceive and *know* it and will you not give heed to it? I will even make a way in the wilderness and rivers in the desert" (Isaiah 43:19 AMP, emphasis mine). Remember, your life is not about *doing* more. Your life is about *being* more—being more at rest, being more at peace, being more confident in Jesus. He wants to do it all for you. And of course, what He can do for you is far more wonderful than anything you could ever do on your own. Psalm 143:8 is a prayer you can take with you 24/7: "Cause me to hear thy lovingkindness in the morning; for in thee do I trust: cause me to *know* the way wherein I should walk; for I lift up my soul unto thee" (emphasis mine).

There is never a reason to feel forsaken when you know for sure that Jesus is with you. He promised that He would never leave you or forsake you. What does the word *never* mean? That's right; it means *not ever!* Build your inner strength on this promise from Psalm 9:10: "They that *know* thy name will put their trust in thee: for thou, LORD, hast not forsaken them that seek thee" (emphasis mine).

What a great truth to stand on when life doesn't make sense! This doesn't suggest that you won't experience times of difficulty or challenge. But you can always be confident, even when you do go through hard places, that the challenges will work for you and not against you because Romans 8:28 assures us: "We *know* that all things work together for good to them that love God, to them who are the called according to his purpose" (emphasis mine).

I want to be found believing God, like Abraham believed God. When faced with challenging circumstances, Abraham did not waver in his faith nor was he unsettled in any way. Regardless of what the situation looked like, Abraham was not moved, but he believed God, taking Him at His word: "He staggered not at the promises of God through unbelief; but was strong in faith, giving glory to God; and being fully persuaded that, what he had promised, he was able also to perform" (Romans 4:20-21).

Do you remember that in the introduction I told you about my first experience with flying first class? Do you recall my saying that I have flown coach and first class but flying first class is a whole lot better? I can also say that I've lived a good portion of my life doubting and second-guessing the Lord's promises to me. But now that I've read His word and I know by experience that He will do just as He said He would, now that I have tasted and seen for myself just how good He is, there's no way I'll be content with anything less. Fully trusting Him is a whole lot better than not trusting Him. No, I'm not perfect. Yes, learning to trust is a process. Some days, having faith feels like being blindfolded. Would you agree? But I'd rather take Jesus by the hand and walk blindly into an unknown future than be in control of my own destiny any day of the week. I can tell you now, what a disaster that would be. Now this girl can sing with confidence, "I have decided to follow Jesus. No turning back. No turning back."

Are you fully persuaded that God will do what He has promised He will do? Have you made up your mind that you will believe God beyond any shadow of a doubt? Let me encourage you to revisit the five landmarks we've talked about throughout the book and keep them in your heart as a reminder to put your faith completely in Christ. My prayer is that as you do, you will be reminded all over again just how faithful and trustworthy God really is. If you're anything at all like me, you'll probably need to be reminded before this day has even ended. In the meantime, I invite you to join me in celebrating what we know for sure. We've repeated this chorus again and again throughout our time together, and I ask you to join me for the grand finale. This is one moment that this alto is happy to be singing to the choir because my faith is increased just knowing that you are standing with me. Whether you sing on pitch or make a joyful noise, find your voice and join right in.

Declare that you will no longer be controlled by your circumstances, no matter what you come up against. Proclaim that you will not be moved by your feelings but be motivated by your faith in Jesus. He will help you carry out His plan and purpose for your life. And when you know Jesus, the One who has given you all these promises and more, you already know what really matters most. Proclaim this with me one more time:

There is a God in Heaven
And I am in His plan
He will forsake me never
My life is in His hands.
His boundless love will lead me
As long as time endures
Oh, this I know
This I know for sure

Amen? Amen.

NOTES

PART 1. THERE IS A GOD IN HEAVEN

1. James Cowden Wallace, "There's Not a Star Whose Twinkling Light," in *The Psalmist: A New Collection of Hymns for the Use of Baptist Churches*, ed. Baron Stow and S. F. Smith (Boston: Gould, Kendall, and Lincoln, 1843), no. 126.

CHAPTER 1. EMBRACING A DEFINING MOMENT

1. Ravi Zacharias, *The Grand Weaver: How God Shapes Us Through the Events of Our Lives* (Grand Rapids: Zondervan, 2010), 38–40.

CHAPTER 2. ESTABLISHING CONFIDENCE IN GOD

1. Charles Spurgeon, "Daniel Facing the Lions' Den," on The Spurgeon Archive, accessed May 8, 2013, www.spurgeon.org/sermons/1154.htm.

PART 2. AND I AM IN HIS PLAN

1. Anonymous, "Lord, Help Me to Resign," in *The Psalmist: A New Collection of Hymns for the Use of the Baptist Churches*, ed. Baron Stow and S. F. Smith (Boston: Gould, Kendall, and Lincoln, 1843), no. 668.

CHAPTER 5. DEMONSTRATING GOD'S CHARACTER

1. Ralph Waldo Emerson, *Emerson on Transcendentalism*, ed. Edward L. Ericson (New York: Continuum, 2002), 60.
2. Babbie Mason, "With All My Heart," © 1990 Word Music, LLC (ASCAP).
3. "Your Walk Talks," words and music by Rodney Griffin and Babbie Mason. Copyright 2011. Songs of Greater Vision/BMI. Praise and Worship Works/ASCAP.

CHAPTER 6. PURSUING GOD'S PURPOSE

1. Tony Sutherland, *Graceworks* (Atlanta: Tony Sutherland Ministries, 2011), emphasis in original.

PART 3: HE WILL FORSAKE ME NEVER

1. Thomas Moore and Thomas Hastings (stanza 3), "Come, Ye Disconsolate," in *The United Methodist Hymnal* (Nashville: The United Methodist Publishing House, 1989), no. 510.

CHAPTER 7. IN THE MEAN TIMES

1. Edward Mote, "My Hope Is Built," in *The United Methodist Hymnal* (Nashville: The United Methodist Publishing House, 1989), no. 368.
2. Jim Cymbala, *Fresh Wind, Fresh Fire* (Grand Rapids: Zondervan, 1997), 167.

PART 4. MY LIFE IS IN HIS HANDS

1. Josiah Conder, "Lord, My Times Are in Thy Hand," in *The National Baptist Hymnal*, 5th rev. ed., ed. R. H. Boyd and William Rosborough (Nashville: National Baptist Pub. Board, 1904), no. 462.

CHAPTER 10. THE PASSION OF FAITH

1. Babbie Mason and Turner Lawton, "Stay Up on the Wall." Copyright 1990 BMM Music, Praise & Worship Works (ASCAP).
2. William James quoted in "The Pragmatic Test" by M. T. McMillan, *Harper's Weekly* 58 (April 18, 1914): 11, http://books.google.com/books?id=1pw0AQAAMAAJ&pg=RA3-PA1&dq=harper's+weekly+1914+pragmatic+test&hl=en&sa=X&ei=gTRkUYnVM4208QSUrYGYCQ&ved=0CEUQ6AEwAw#v=onepage&q=harper's%20weekly%201914%20pragmatic%20test&f=false.

CHAPTER 11. THE PROMISE OF FAITH

1. Ernest Bacon, *Spurgeon: Heir of the Puritans* (Arlington Heights, IL: Christian Liberty Press, 1996), 114.
2. Adrian Rogers, video, "Six Principles to Fortify Faith," *Love Worth Finding*, November 11, 2012, www.lightsource.com/ministry/love-worth-finding/six-principles-to-fortify-faith-307514.html.

PART 5: HIS BOUNDLESS LOVE WILL LEAD ME AS LONG AS TIME ENDURES

1. Francis Scott Key, "Lord, with Glowing Heart I'd Praise Thee," in *The Psalmist: A New Collection of Hymns for the Use of Baptist Churches*, ed. Richard Fuller (Boston: Gould, Kendall, and Lincoln, 1849), p. 724.
2. Babbie Mason, "Standing in the Gap" © 1993 Word Music, LLC (ASCAP) and May Sun Publishing (ASCAP).

CHAPTER 14. THE GOD WHO WILLINGLY FORGIVES

1. *Matthew Henry's Concise Commentary on The Bible.* www.biblegateway.com/resources/commentaries/Matthew-Henry/Luke/Prodigal-Son-Wickedness.
2. William Rees, "Here Is Love," trans. William Edwards, *The Baptist Book of Praise* (1900).

CHAPTER 15. THE GOD WHO GOES OUT OF HIS WAY

1. James C. Whittaker, *We Thought We Heard the Angels Sing* (New York, E. P. Dutton, 1943).

PART 6. OH, THIS I KNOW; THIS I KNOW FOR SURE

1. William Wrangham, "To Thee, My Righteous King and Lord," in *The Psalmist: A New Collection of Hymns for the Use of the Baptist Churches*, ed. Baron Stowe and S. F. Smith (Boston: Gould, Kendall, and Lincoln, 1843), no. 112.

ABOUT THE AUTHOR

Babbie Mason is a Dove Award–winning, Grammy-nominated American gospel singer and songwriter, whose concert appearances have taken her across the United States and the globe. Inducted into the Christian Music Hall of Fame in 2010, she has appeared at numerous Billy Graham Crusades worldwide, Women of Faith Conferences, the Grammy Awards, and Carnegie Hall. She is at home on the national stage, having performed with such Christian music favorites such as CeCe Winans, Bill and Gloria Gaither, and the Brooklyn Tabernacle Choir, and she has shared the platform with such notable people as presidents Jimmy Carter, Gerald Ford, George H. W. Bush, and George W. Bush; former First Lady Barbara Bush; Jeff Foxworthy; and Bill Cosby.

A mentor to upstarts in the music ministry through her music conferences, the Inner Circle, a tireless women's conference speaker, a worship leader through her Embrace: A Worship Celebration for Women and This I Know for Sure worship concerts, an adjunct professor of songwriting at Lee and Liberty Universities, a television talk show host of *Babbie's House*, and a published author of popular books and Bible studies, Babbie Mason is a woman with a passion to uplift others with her gifts.

The parents of two adult sons, Babbie and her husband, Charles Mason, live on a farm in west Georgia.

Powerful Anthems and Worship Songs
to inspire you through the *This I Know for Sure* Bible Study

As you listen to and sing these memorable songs that accompany the themes of the book and the six-week Bible study, *This I Know For Sure*, you will be reminded that God loves you, He will never forsake you, and He has a wonderful plan for your life. Each song dovetails perfectly with the theme and serves as the foundation for a worship celebration every church will enjoy.

This I Know For Sure

Hear these songs on the CD or LIVE in Babbie Mason's faith affirming worship concert, *This I Know For Sure*.

Find out more at www.babbie.com

Learn to Live a Life of *Unshakable Faith*
with a new Bible study from Babbie Mason

Do you desire a rock-solid faith to believe God for the challenges you are facing, regardless of how you may feel?

This 6-week Bible study by award-winning Gospel singer/songwriter and Bible teacher Babbie Mason challenges you to make up your mind to believe God's word regardless of your feelings or circumstances.

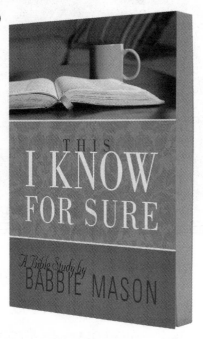

Whether you are wrestling with questions or fears; struggling in your relationships; or facing a health, financial, or other crisis; these principles will enable you to trust God with your doubts, cease your wavering, and drive a spiritual stake of faith into the ground.

Participant Book
9781426772450
$14.99

Leader Guide
9781426772467
$12.99

DVD Study
9781426772474
$49.99

Preview Book
9781426772481
$1.99

Leader Kit
9781426775697
$79.99

Uplifting and *God-honoring* Music

Inspired by her warm and encouraging book, *Embraced By God*, each song on the CD *Embrace* resonates with the themes of the book and the eight-week Bible study, underscoring the powerful messages of God's grace,

acceptance, and forgiveness. The songs from the CD also serve as the backdrop for Babbie Mason's worship concert, *Embrace: A Worship Celebration for Women.*

Discover Who You Are and Whose You Are

Embark on a twenty-one day journey to receive God's embrace. As Babbie Mason shares her personal story of how she came to understand how very much God loves her, not as a singer or teacher but as His child, she will help you accept that same love and grow in confidence in your faith.

9781426741340
$15.99

Share the *Embraced by God* Experience with Your Small Group

This 8-week study from Babbie Mason will help each woman in your small group know she is loved, accepted, and valued by God. Drawing on her own personal faith journey, Babbie will equip you to accept God's unfailing love and claim seven biblical promises that will deepen your relationship with your Savior and with other women.

Participant Book	Leader Guide	DVD Study
9781426754418	9781426754425	9781426754425
$14.99	$12.99	$39.99
Preview Book	Leader Kit	
9781426757747	9781426777943	
$1.99	$69.99	

Purchase the music of Babbie Mason at www.babbie.com

EVERYTHING
An inspiring collection of worship songs written and delivered as only Babbie Mason can. Includes: *Everything, Let Your Fire Fall, Come Thou Fount, Strong Tower, God Will Open Up the Windows*, and more.

MY BEST SO FAR, VOLUME ONE
Features the timeless classics that have made Babbie Mason a quintessential gospel music artist. Includes: *Each One Reach One, God Has Another Plan, With All My Heart, Love is the More Excellent Way, All Rise, Standing in the Gap*, and more.

MY BEST SO FAR, VOLUME TWO
More classic favorites from Babbie Mason, this collection features songs the church has come to love such as: *Pray On, Trust His Heart, It Must Be Love, Carry On, Jesus the One and Only, To the Cross, Stop By the Church, Shine the Light, In All of His Glory* and more.

CHUCK ROAST (DVD)
This LIVE concert pays tribute to love, marriage, and Babbie's husband, Charles, letting you on the inside of their marriage of more than three decades. The contents will cause side-splitting, hilarious, and contagious laughter as you get to know Babbie, Charles, and the Mason family up close and personal.

TREASURED MEMORIES
Paying beautiful homage to the African American worship experience, this LIVE worship service, recorded in Babbie Mason's hometown of Jackson, Michigan, features the soulful, heartfelt hymns and spiritual songs of days gone by, featuring The Barrett Sisters, Willie Rogers, Inez Andrews, Georgie Wade, and more. Songs include *Near the Cross, Come and Go to That Land, Old Ship of Zion, Yes, Jesus Loves Me, What A Fellowship*, and more.

Embrace: A Worship Celebration for Women, is a ninety-minute, interactive concert with a purpose. In an atmosphere of worship and an attitude of joy, Babbie Mason invites women to step away from life's responsibilities, breathe out, let go of the challenges they face, and receive the love, validation, and comfort that every woman needs. At every *Embrace* concert, women experience exciting worship music, God-honoring testimonies, the fellowship of Christian sisterhood, and a huge dose of encouragement, all in an atmosphere where women can encounter the unconditional love of God.

Babbie Mason says, "I've had the privilege of being a part of women's ministry from the local church to the national stage for a long time now. And wherever I go, I meet women who are in desperate need of encouragement. Too often women are discouraged, depressed, and defeated. Women need to know that they really matter to God, and that He has a great big plan and we're all in it. I'm so honored that God would give me the music and the opportunity to lead women in worship at each of these encounters. *Embrace: A Worship Celebration For Women* was created to give women the opportunity to bask in the deepend of God's love and receive healing for our hearts."

Inspired by her new and uplifting book, *Embraced By God,* Babbie Mason presents the companion CD *Embrace.* Encouraging and God-honoring, each song resonates with the themes of the book, underscoring the powerful messages of God's grace, acceptance, and forgiveness. The songs from the CD also serve as a backdrop for Babbie Mason's worship concert, *Embrace: A Worship Celebration for Women.*

Send some love to a special someone with Babbie Mason's *Embrace* note cards. Each blank card allows you to write your own sentiments of hope and encouragement. Each box contains twelve cards and envelopes.

For more information go to www.babbie.com.

THE INNER CIRCLE

Babbie Mason and her husband, Charles, host their own exciting music conference, The Inner Circle, drawing on almost three decades of music ministry and business experience to encourage and mentor those desiring to jump-start their own endeavors. The Inner Circle is packed full of tools and tips for launching a music ministry, writing great lyrics and music, making a great CD on a not-so-great budget, vocal care, critiques, and internet marketing techniques. Babbie features many of her friends in the music industry who join her for this encouraging weekend conference. Hear from producers, writers, arrangers, vocal coaches, entertainment attorneys, web masters, and Christian artists. Guests have included Helen Baylor, Carol Cymbala (director of the Brooklyn Tabernacle Choir), Charles Billingsley, Ron Kenoly, Morris Chapman, Pastor William Murphy, Kenn Mann, Donna Douglas, Turner Lawton, Eulalia King, Cheryl Rogers, and more!

Find out more at www.babbie.com